Change Your Life T

The Ultimate Guide to Motivation, Success & Happiness

By Lewis David

WinsPress.com 2019

Text Copyright © Lewis David 2019

All rights reserved. No part of this publication may be reproduced, or transmitted in any form or by any means, electronic or otherwise, without written permission from the author.

Legal & Disclaimer

The information contained in this book is not designed to replace or take the place of any form of medicine or professional medical advice. The information contained in this book has been compiled from sources deemed reliable, and it is accurate to the best of the Author's knowledge; however, the Author cannot guarantee its accuracy and validity and cannot be held liable for any errors or omissions. Changes are periodically made to this book. You must consult your doctor or get professional medical advice before using any of the suggested remedies, techniques, or information in this book. Upon using the information contained in this book, you agree to hold harmless the Author from and against any damages, costs, and expenses, including any legal fees potentially resulting from the application of any of the information provided by this guide. This disclaimer applies to any damages or injury caused by the use and application, whether directly or indirectly, of any advice or information presented, whether for breach of contract, tort, negligence, personal injury, criminal intent, or under any other cause of action. You agree to accept all risks of using the information presented inside this book. You need to consult a professional medical practitioner before embarking on any program or information in this book.

About the Author

I am a therapist, trained in the UK healthcare system. I have worked with thousands of people in hospital outpatient services and the community, both in private and state-funded projects.

I am now a full-time author and founded the publishing house WinsPress.com. I'm married with adult children and live in England and Portugal.

Dedication:

To my inspirational wife, Antonia.

"You begin by always expecting good things to happen."

Tom Hopkins

Contents

Change Your Life Today

Can you really change your life today?

Yes, you can. Today and every day – if you embrace change rather than hide from it. This book is about how you can make change a force for good in your life and achieve greater success and happiness.

You may want to get slimmer and fitter, find a better job, overcome an addiction, pass an exam, win the respect of your peers, start a business, stop self-destructive habits, live longer, win at a sport, move on from past pain, overcome anxiety, learn a language, find the perfect partner, or you might simply have a yearning for a more fulfilling life.

Whatever you want to achieve, you will find not only inspiration in these pages but also effective techniques you can put into practice right now – today.

As a counselor, I have worked with thousands of clients to help them experience positive change. In the course of this work, I have seen certain principles succeed time and again. These have worked with all kinds of people and in all sorts of different situations. The success rates have been phenomenal. Everyone who has stuck with the principles you will discover in this book has succeeded.

And I do mean everyone.

None of the concepts in this book is complicated. Mysticism or great leaps of faith are not required. You will learn solid ways to deal with your difficulties or achieve your ambitions, whatever they might be. All you have to do is apply these concepts and you will change your life for the better.

And the adventure starts with your truest desires.

It All Begins with Desire

Have you ever wanted something, only to find out when you got it that it failed to do for you what you thought it would?

Maybe you wanted a certain kind of relationship, but when you found it, you still felt unfulfilled. Perhaps it was a dream job, but when you got it, you found it unsatisfying and you wanted to do something else. Maybe you wanted a possession that you thought would make you feel happy, but by the time you got it, your mind had already moved on to the next thing you thought would make you feel better. Perhaps you heard of a drug that you thought might transform how you felt, but after you took it, life seemed even worse. Maybe you wanted to live in a certain place, only to discover that when you moved there, you still felt empty inside.

If something like this has happened to you, then in all probability the reason was that what you thought you wanted was unaligned with your deep-down desires. So, when you got what you thought you wanted, it didn't light up your life as you thought it would. Instead, it was a disappointment because your underlying desire was still unmet.

Or have you ever thought that you wanted something but just somehow couldn't muster the motivation to go after it? You tried to use motivational techniques but procrastinated anyway. Maybe you even thought there was something wrong with you, that you were lacking in some way.

If this has happened, then it's likely that the same lack of alignment was the problem. You couldn't get the motivation to go for your goal because, deep down inside of you, on an unconscious level, you knew it wouldn't meet your true desire.

This lack of alignment is an easy trap to fall into. It happens all the time. It has certainly happened to me. Common reasons for this are:

What we think we want is, in reality, what someone else wants. We are doing something to please other people.

We are doing something because of social conditioning and what we think society expects.

We do things because that's the way it's always been done, without questioning if it's the right way for us.

In other words, we do things because we think we should do something. For instance, my wife once thought she should do a law degree. It seemed to make sense as it was a good degree to have. But it wasn't her desire, so her heart wasn't in it. After a year she abandoned it and studied history instead, which she enjoyed, and got that degree.

When I was in my twenties, I thought I should get into IT work as the money seemed good, so I set up a business designing bespoke databases. The business made money right away. But I had to give it up after a year because the work made me unhappy. It simply wasn't my desire at all. I really couldn't have cared less about databases. I was just doing it for the money, which rarely works out well in the long term.

If the word "should" is involved, you can be pretty sure you are doing something that is unaligned with your true desire.

This can have disastrous outcomes. For example:

People end up in the wrong career because they are trying to fulfill their parents' ambitions for them rather than doing what would bring them joy and deep satisfaction.

Some find themselves trapped in unhappy marriages because they think that they need a partner who fits certain stereotypes rather than someone they truly love.

Others live a lifestyle that is not natural for them and brings them unhappiness because they are afraid of stepping outside the social norms they were brought up with.

Some lose unhealthy amounts of weight, or even get surgery, trying to look like the models in airbrushed images they see in magazines, tragically not realizing that they looked great all along.

Still others turn to prescription or illicit drugs and, in the end, find they need to keep taking them just to feel normal.

So, before you begin the task of changing your life for the better, you need to know from the outset that your goal is aligned with your deep-down desire. Otherwise, disappointment or worse will surely follow. Achieving a goal that you never truly desired will sap your energy and resources, leaving you feeling empty or even desperate.

However, you can use a simple technique to test your goal and check that it is genuinely your true desire. I call it the "Why is that?" strategy. I have used this successfully with many of my therapy clients, and I also use it on myself regularly. I suggest you use it before you get deeper into this book. This is how it works:

Ask yourself, "What do you want?" Then, when you have answered that question, ask yourself, "Why is that?" When you have the answer, ask again, "Why is that?" Keep asking the question for each answer you come up with until you are sure you have drilled right down to your deepest desire.

I will illustrate how this works with a real-life example. I had a new client called Sam come to see me. Sam was a 27-year-old, self-employed builder who lived with his wife and their young child. Things were going well. He was happy in his relationship. They lived in a fine apartment that Sam had lovingly refurbished. He had all the work he needed. The money was pouring in and he had taken on staff. There was, however, one big snag: Sam was spending all his spare income on his cocaine habit. He had come to me for counseling.

With this type of problem, the counselor will usually try to help the client to focus on a positive activity to replace their habit. So, when I initially spoke to Sam, I asked him to think about what he really wanted and then tell me what it was when we next met. This is what happened:

"So, Sam, have you chosen a positive goal for yourself?" I asked at the start of our next meeting.

Sam nodded and said: "I want to buy one of the white houses by the park." I knew the houses he meant. They were imposing, expensive, and much bigger than Sam needed for his small family.

"Really?" I said. "I thought you loved your apartment."

"I do," Sam replied. "But I want to move."

"Why is that?" I asked.

"It would be great to have a big place when my relatives come to visit," he said. "We have a family get-together at my place a couple of times a year. It would really impress them."

"You want a bigger house to impress your relatives?" I asked. "Why is that?"

"Well," he hesitated, "it's just that sometimes I think they look down on me."

"Really? I asked again. "Why is that?"

Sam started to open up. He explained how he had an older brother called Darren, who Sam thought was the bright one in the family. Darren had got a good university degree, gone into banking and done financially well for himself.

"I guess if I got a house more like his, the family would see me as his equal," said Sam.

Now we were getting down to what Sam's real desire was. It wasn't the new house at all, as he was happy in his apartment. What he truly desired was to feel as valued as his brother.

"So," I responded, "what have people in your family said to make you think that they don't see you as equal?"

16

"Well, nothing really," he said, uncertainly. "But I guess with him being a banker and me a builder..."

I could see that the problem was not in the family's perception of Sam, but Sam's perception of his own status. Getting a bigger house was unlikely to change that. Over the next couple of sessions, we worked on Sam's feelings of self-worth.

Sam began to see that what he had done as a builder was massively to his credit, and the idea that his family looked down on him was an illusion of his own making. Over the following few months, he turned his focus to expanding his business, which in turn built up his self-esteem, and his cocaine habit faded as he no longer needed a drug to feel good.

You can see from Sam's story how simple but powerful the "Why is that?" strategy is. It can be a revelation to people when they realize what they truly desire. In my exchange with Sam, I used "Why is that?" three times and I was quickly able to uncover what Sam's true desire was, which Sam hadn't seen himself.

The "Why is that?" technique is versatile. You can use it deliberately with yourself. When you find yourself trying to decide what you should do, keep asking "Why is that?" until you get to the truth. And when you have established what that is, you can proceed with confidence, knowing what you are doing is in line with your true desire, optimizing your chance of a satisfying and successful outcome.

Using "Why is that?" might surprise you, as your subconscious mind gives up secrets that had been hiding from your conscious mind. You can also use it in a caring way to help people in your life. It works on all levels. You can use it with your spouse or your parents. Equally, you can use it with your children as part of your parenting skills. It is also invaluable with work colleagues. If you are in any kind of management role, it will help you understand your employees' needs. But conversely, you can use it with your manager to better understand what your organization requires of you.

However, I will add a couple of caveats to this strategy. Firstly, if you use "Why is that?" to drill down to your true desire, and it shows you something dark, something that could hurt you or other people, such as a desire to harm yourself in some way, then you must get professional help. Secondly, if you use it with others, do so helpfully and compassionately rather than trying to catch people out.

But what if you are still unclear about what you want? Let's look at that next.

But I Don't Know What I Want

Some people have found that using the "Why is that?" strategy doesn't work initially because they can't answer the first "What do you want?" question. Most of the clients I have worked with in my professional life as a counselor have wanted change. But many of them were constantly frustrated because they didn't know what the change was that they were looking for. They didn't know what they wanted – they just knew they wanted something better.

This can be a massive issue for people who pass from year to year without any sense of direction. They go around and around in circles in their minds, trying to find the answer. I have had clients in tears of frustration because they just can't decide what they want. Some people go through their entire lives in this miserable state.

I have realized that there can be different reasons why people find themselves in this situation. The first reason is being overwhelmed. This happens when so much needs fixing in someone's life that they are mind-blown about where to start and end up taking no action at all. They are bewildered about what to prioritize. Imagine having multiple fires burning in your life but having only one bucket of water. Which fire should you put out? What about the rest?

I've found this is usually the case with people I have counseled for self-destructive behavior. Let's take excessive gambling as an example. They learn to stop the compulsion to gamble, but then find that they have to get on with dealing with the trouble the gambling had caused, like debts, broken relationships, lost housing, and ruptured careers. These clients often find they are frozen by indecision. They have ended their self-destructive behavior, but they still have multiple fires burning in their lives.

Another situation might be where a client has already achieved a goal, and this has left them directionless. A common situation I have encountered, for example, is where someone has worked for years for retirement. This goal has kept them motivated and given their life meaning. Then the golden day comes when they can retire and for a few weeks or months, it's wonderful – they can do what they like.

After a while, however, they feel lost because their life lacks focus. They realize they need a goal once more but simply can't decide what. In the past, they didn't have to think about it. The goal was clear: retirement. But now they can't find anything which gives them that same compelling drive, and they miss that.

Other clients I have worked with have had their lives turned upside down by a sudden change in circumstances, such as unemployment, relationship break-up, or a medical condition that has meant the person can no longer do what they used to. It leaves them feeling directionless and lost.

Many people spend years, even decades, waiting for that magical day when the clouds part and their true meaning is revealed to them like a blinding beam of sunlight. However, if you are one of those people, I have bad news: you might wait a long time; you might die waiting.

But there is a fix.

In this chapter, I shall explain some different strategies that I have seen work for many clients. Take a look at these and see if there is one that can help you in your life.

To begin, take a piece of paper and brainstorm with yourself (or maybe with the help of someone you trust) anything you might want to do. Don't worry about how crazy your ideas might be, just get writing. Make the longest list that you can. Keep going until you feel you have exhausted your mind of ideas.

Once you have done that, give each item on the list a score out of five for how important you think it is. Be careful that you are rating it as how important you think it is to you, not how important it is to someone else. Do you remember what we have already said about things you think you should do? Where the word "should" is involved, it usually means that you are doing something for someone else or because of someone else's values. You are unlikely to get a good outcome because it will be someone else's desire rather than yours.

Having done that, go through your list again and give each item another score out of five, this time for how urgent it is to you. Be careful to understand that important and urgent mean two quite different things. For example, if I want my car to work, I would give putting fuel in the tank five for importance. But if I already have a full tank, I would only give it one for urgency. If I had half a tank, I would give it maybe three for urgency. If the indicator was on the red and the engine was running on fumes, I would give it a five for urgency. Just because something is important doesn't mean it's always urgent, and vice-versa.

Now go through your list again and add your scores for importance and urgency together for each item. You now have a total score out of ten for each item. The item that has the highest score out of ten would be a great place for you to be focusing your attention.

This system for prioritizing works on many levels. It can be used to sort out major life priorities, or it works just as well for short-term focus, such as optimizing your work schedule. It's also really useful if you have a particular project happening, such as starting a business or buying a property. You start with addressing the item with the highest score then work down the list in order of the score.

The feedback clients have given me for this system has always been positive. It cuts through the confusion. As one client said to me, it gives "instant clarity."

Another system I have seen work well for people trying to get focused on the big issues in their lives is this: instead of asking yourself what you want, try asking yourself what you fear most.

We all have fears. The most successful person you know has fears. The most confident person you know has fears. Having rational fears is healthy, keeping you safe from real dangers. Even irrational fears such as phobias can be quite harmless unless they are extreme.

So, what do you fear? What do you desire not to happen? Maybe loneliness, ill health, business failure, old age, disease – whatever it is, put it to the "Why is that?" test to see if there is more going on than you consciously realized.

When you have your answer, you can start turning your fear to your advantage. To do this, ask yourself what you could do to take yourself as far as possible away from your fear. For example, if your fear is being overwhelmed by financial worries, your aim might be to downsize your commitments. If you fear ill health, your aim might be to change your eating and activity habits. If you fear loneliness, your aim might be to join an organization where you will meet like-minded people. And so on.

Finally, another way to address the problem of lack of focus is to start by looking at what you're good at, or have the potential to be good at. Everyone has some sort of talent. What's yours?

If nothing instantly springs to mind, think carefully, look at things you have done in the past that have gone okay, and get together a list. Maybe it could be something you have done before but stopped doing, or something you do now but not in a committed way. Is there something that you could be focusing on that you could get terrific at?

The theme of this book is about using change for success and happiness. If there is something that you can focus on and enjoy success with, happiness will usually follow. We all like the feeling of doing something well, whatever that is.

Using the ideas that you have read about so far, you should be able to find out what, for you, is your desire.

Next, you need a path.

The Path

A few years ago, the hospital where I worked wanted me to run a series of therapeutic groups for some people who had been attending outpatient counseling. Although they had finished their program of counseling, the clients still needed some motivational support to help them move forward. As they had varying needs, it wasn't appropriate to focus on specific issues. Instead, I needed to structure a program that would work for everyone. The program that evolved for these clients was super-successful.

It became known as The Path.

I have since used The Path with many clients, who have all responded well to it. I have also used it on myself. Indeed, I am using it right now. I think the great strength of The Path is that it's clear, easy to understand and follow. Consequently, it doesn't get forgotten about in the hurly-burly of daily life, which is the weakness of many self-development programs.

Having a carefully crafted program is great, but it needs to be something that you can still remember when you are upset, going through challenging times, or when you have just been hit by a seemingly random event. More than that, a successful program needs to be something you can fall back on when life is tough as well as on good days. The Path achieves this. It's simple, but it's profound in what it can achieve.

This is how it works:

Imagine that what you want to achieve is on a distant hill. Between you and it, there are hills, valleys, forests, and rivers. You don't know how to get to your goal on that distant hill. You can see it, but you fear you could get lost trying to get there and maybe never reach it. The task is daunting.

But then, as if by magic, a path suddenly appears at your feet, and it runs through the countryside all the way to your goal on that distant hill. Suddenly the task is no longer daunting. You simply need to follow The Path and you will be all right. You will reach your goal. You feel motivated and inspired because you realize that as long as you keep moving forward and stay on The Path, you cannot fail.

That's right. You cannot fail. Stay on The Path and you simply have to reach your goal.

No other outcome is possible.

How good is that?

Path is an acronym. It stands for "Planning and Total Honesty". Let's start with your plan.

Planning.

Your plan needs to contain a simple, achievable Daily Action that compounded over time will move you to your goal. This Daily Action is the minimum that you need to do to keep you moving forward every day. Think of this repeated Daily Action as being a step along The Path. When you have taken enough steps, you will have reached your ggoal. Let's look at some examples.

I mentioned that I am using The Path right now. I am applying The Path to writing the book that you are holding. The idea of writing a book can be overwhelming. It's a big undertaking. It would be very easy for me to procrastinate and never get around to finishing it. I could keep coming up with excuses. I could tell myself that something else needs to be done right now, or I need to do another thing first. But there is always stuff that needs to be done. So, I need to take that Daily Action to move me along my Path every day, or I will never finish this book.

My Daily Action is simply to get to my computer at 9.00 in the morning and before I do anything else, write at least 500 words. That's not a lot. I know I can achieve that, as I usually write far more. In fact, I have already written 500 words this morning in my first half hour at my computer. I'll probably go on to write much more today.

On another day, however, I might feel less inspired, and writing those 500 words is hard work and might take a few hours. But to achieve my Daily Action, I must persist and do it. Then, even if I only ever achieved my minimum target of 500 words daily, I would write my book. It might take a few months, but I would get there. No other outcome is possible.

Let's take another example. Let's say you want to lose weight. You have realized that if you ditch all the junk food and follow a low-fat, wholefood diet, you will lose weight. It's inevitable because your caloric intake will drop significantly, even if you eat as much in terms of quantity as you do now (I'll be discussing this more in a later chapter on weight management). So, your Daily Action is to eat as much of that type of food as you wish. That doesn't sound too difficult.

If you want to become less anxious, your Daily Action could be to do 10 minutes of mindfulness every day. It doesn't sound much, but the cumulative effect over a few weeks would be significant.

If you want to become more successful as a salesperson, committing to a Daily Action of starting work 15 minutes earlier and making 2 extra sales calls per day would inevitably increase your success rate. That's an extra 40 calls per month, which is likely to translate into more sales.

Total Honesty.

Planning is only part of it. To stay on your Path, you must be 100% honest with yourself. It's tempting to justify to ourselves why we should not do something we had planned to do today. Usually, this is just excusing procrastination.

So, next time you find yourself thinking this way, be honest and ask yourself: Is that the truth or just an excuse? For example, if your mind is talking you into not doing something because, let's say, you feel little unwell, ask yourself: truth or excuse? Am I really that unwell, or is it just an excuse to be lazy?

Focus on your Daily Action.

Does your mind focus on the future? Are you prone to questioning your plans? Does your mind keep coming up with "what if?" scenarios that shake your confidence? I know my mind does if I let it. The solution is just to focus on doing your Daily Action, and then you are done for the day. You don't need to project ahead. As long as you have taken your Daily Action, you know that you have advanced along your Path, and that's all that matters. You are closer to achieving your goal.

Check Where Your Feet Are.

Another way to make sure you're on your Path is to keep an eye on where your feet are. I am not talking figuratively here. I mean literally – what are your feet up to?

For instance, if you are on a diet and your feet are walking towards a pizza restaurant, are you about to step off your Path? If you have decided to stay out of the life of an ex-partner, why are your feet walking down the street where he lives? If you have resolved to go for a run every morning and your feet are still in bed 20 minutes after the alarm went off, are you still on your Path? If you have resolved to have a booze-free month, why are your feet walking down the alcohol lane at the supermarket?

Rest Days.

You should decide before you start on your Path whether it is appropriate to take rest days and, if so, when. If you are following a fitness program, then rest days are usually part of the program. If your target is work or study-related, then having days off would be healthy. I am giving myself weekends off from writing this book to keep my mind fresh, so I only do my Daily Action on weekdays. But if you are on a diet, you should decide whether you are going for it 100% or if you will have days off. And you need to decide this in advance. Otherwise, you might be dishonest with yourself about your motives.

Now, let's look at how you can apply The Path to what you want in your life.

Following the Instructions

How many books in the self-development genre have you read? Is this the first? Probably not. More likely you have a little library of self-development on your shelf or downloaded onto your reading device. And from those books, how many have had a program that you have thoroughly followed? Any? Or have you simply started the next book?

Do you have books that promise you can achieve great things if you follow a particular plan for 7 days, or 21 days, or 30 days, or whatever the time scale might be? Have you ever faithfully followed those plans to the letter, for the specified time, and achieved the promised outcome?

No, me neither.

Until I did.

Then I found I could change my life – by choice, not by chance.

As a young man, I always tried to find my own way to do everything. I would always go for the shortcut. I would try to achieve the most with the least amount of effort. No wonder my life became chaotic. I was constantly trying to think of new solutions instead of just doing the obvious thing which worked.

I never followed instructions. I just couldn't be bothered. Anyway, I thought didn't need to. I thought I was clever. You can imagine what my attempts at self-assembly furniture were like: I always had lots of screws left over and would wonder why the wardrobe I had just constructed fell apart when you hung your coat in it.

But over the years, I have gradually learnt that trying to do things my way might not always be the smart way. I struggled to make grades at school because I didn't think I needed to do the work. I thought I could rely on my natural ability. I was wrong.

Later, when I trained to be a therapist, I discovered that if I actually turned up and did the work, I would get the qualification. This was a revelation to me. And it wasn't painful – it was fun.

I had finally discovered the power of putting my ego to one side and simply following a Path. It pained me to accept that I wasn't the genius I thought I was, and that I just caused myself disappointment and frustration. But I also discovered that life wasn't as complicated as I thought, either. It had been me all along who was making it complicated. I finally started following the instructions, and it changed my life.

Even now, when I'm faced with something new that I want to achieve, my mind tells me to do it my way.

But at last, I finally know better. Instead of trying to be a genius, I use the genius of other people who have successfully trod the same path before me. In other words, I look for a plan that has been proven to work.

Here's an example from my life:

I had always detested running. When I was at school, the activity I hated most was cross-country running. I loathed feeling sweaty and breathless and, worst of all, being poor at doing it. That didn't sit well with the high opinion I had of myself.

I convinced myself that I must be the wrong body type. All the runners I saw on sports programs were small and slightly built. I, on the other hand, am tall and broadly built. So, I thought, that explained it: I was simply the wrong shape for running. Instead, I got good at sports where my long reach helped, like Badminton. I decided I would leave running to the flyweights.

But then one day not that long ago, I read an article about a program called Couch to 5K. It stated that if you followed this program, in nine weeks you would go from being the proverbial couch potato to being able to run five kilometres (about three miles). At the time, I never even ran five metres, never mind five kilometres. But all you had to do was download the app onto your phone, then run three times a week, following the instructions on your earbuds while you were doing it.

Couch to 5K came from Public Health England, so I knew it would have been well-researched and proven to work. It would be a quality plan that I could commit to.

It said that anyone could learn to run 5K.

Learn?

It had never occurred to me that you learned to run. I guess I had always assumed it was instinctive. That got me interested. At the time, I had been doing a lot of walking to keep fit but felt that I needed to do something more to make progress. So, I decided to commit myself to the nine-week program.

The first session was mostly walking for half an hour, with a few 90 seconds bursts of running mixed in, but even that left me breathless. I felt unsure this was going to work. To go from struggling to run for 90 seconds to being able to run 5K, which would take about half an hour, didn't look likely to happen for me.

But I reminded myself that I had been told that anyone could learn this – and anyone includes me. I just needed to make the effort three times per week and put my faith in the program.

The little voice in my head that always wants me to put my feet up and procrastinate did its best to get me to abandon the plan. Every morning, it tried to talk me into an extra half-hour in bed. Every time there was a single cloud in the sky, it tried to persuade me that a deluge of Biblical proportions was bound to engulf me if I ventured out for my run. Nevertheless, I bought a good pair of running shoes and followed the instructions.

Nine weeks later I could run 5K.

Some people reading this will have always been good at running and will be wondering why I am making a fuss about it. But I can't tell you how amazing it is to me that I can do this, and I go out for a run most days now. It seems like a miracle, but in fact, it's just the power of following a Path and doing the Daily Action (which in the case of Couch to 5K was to run three times a week with four rest days).

It also shows that when you are doing the planning for your Path, using well-researched information that has been proven is the way to go. Don't just make it up yourself. Seek out what has been shown to work and do that.

And stop trying so hard.

In my work as a therapist, I used to despair of clients who constantly told me that they would try. Does that surprise you? Surely you would think that being told that someone was going to try to do something is a good thing, wouldn't you?

No, it's not. The clients who left my consulting room with a cheery "I'll try my best, see you next week," were always the ones who came back the following week with a story of woe and failure. Or even worse, they wouldn't show up for the next meeting because they were embarrassed.

I don't want my clients to tell me they will try – I want them to tell me they have a plan. I want them to tell me what they will do tomorrow, and the next day. I want them to tell me their contingency plan in case of life unexpectedly throwing seemingly random events at them. I want them to keep an eye on where their feet are. I want them to have a Path. They're the winners.

So, when are you going to start on your Path to change your life?

How about today?

Don't Wait Until You're Ready

In the last chapter, I mentioned that little voice in your head. You know the one. It's the voice that tells you that you're wrong, that you are too slow, too fat, too lazy, too dumb, too clever, too young, too old, too tall, too short, too hairy, too bald, too underqualified, too overqualified, too experienced, too inexperienced, and so forth. It's the voice that beats you up when you make a mistake.

Psychologists often call this voice the Inner Critic. It sits in judgment of you all the time. But I think that gives it too much of a sense of authority, which is partly why people get pushed around by this inner voice. They think it's in charge.

I like to think of it as the little voice of your fears. It comes from past pain. It comes from all those times when life has hurt you. It's actually a voice of compassion because it wants you to avoid feeling pain again. It associates change with pain because you have experienced pain in the past when change has randomly been imposed upon you.

So, when you decide you want to make changes, it says: "Whoa, wait a minute. Are you sure about doing that? It would expose you to possible failure, and that hurts. Wouldn't it be better that you carry on doing what you're doing now? You know what that's like. It might not be what you desire, but at least you know what you're going to get."

Sometimes the voice will do a good job and keep you from getting into trouble. But it can also keep you in a situation that you would be best to move on from. It tries to persuade you to stay with what you have, even if what you have is not what you want.

The voice tells you to stay in the same uninspiring job, stay at the same weight, stay with a partner who is hurting you, keep consuming things you know are bad for you, or stay in the same neighborhood although you hate it. The voice argues the case for staying with what is familiar rather than experiencing something new.

Working with clients, I find one of the biggest difficulties in my job is that I am competing with the voice of their Inner Critic. During the hour that I spend with a client, we can get a lot of things agreed upon, and the client goes away with a course of action to make positive changes to their life. But once the client leaves the room, the voice of their Inner Critic starts in their head – and it has all week, until the client next sees me, to sow the seeds of self-doubt in the client's mind.

A week is a long time for the voice to do its worst. And that's what the voice likes best: time to work with. So, it will intrude on your thoughts while you are at work or when you are watching TV. Its favorite trick is to wake you up in the middle of the night and start you worrying.

If you want to make changes in your life, you need to get the upper hand on the voice, or it will sabotage your plans every time. Here's how:

Take some action immediately. Don't wait until you think you're ready – that gives the voice time to sabotage you. You will never be 100% ready, anyway. Make a start. You will take the voice by surprise because you will be taking yourself by surprise. And that will give you something very valuable:

Momentum.

And momentum will crush the voice of your fears.

So, if you were planning to study for a new qualification, get online and sign up now. If you intended to start a healthy eating plan on the first day of next month, start now instead – today. Clear out the cupboards of all your junk food and donate it to the food bank.

When I tried to give up smoking in the past, I always tried to start on a date and time I had decided in advance. It never worked. Then one day, at about eight o'clock in the evening, I suddenly decided to stop. It was so sudden, 10 seconds earlier I had no idea I going to quit. My Inner Critic was completely taken by surprise and kept quiet.

It was one of those random moments in life that I hadn't seen coming. I could have ignored it and carried on smoking, but I decided to go with it. The following morning, when the cravings started to give me a hard time, my Inner Critic had taken time to get over the shock of my sudden action, and it tried to persuade me to smoke. But, by that time, I had already gone 12 hours and I had momentum. I thought – let's get this done. That was in 2012 and I haven't smoked since, which shows the power of not waiting until you're ready and using randomness in your life to your advantage.

When I wrote my first book, a similar thing happened. At the time, I had been carrying out a lot of counseling work at a hospital outpatient facility with problem drinkers. The results had been excellent, and I believed that I had valuable research that I should share with all drinkers in need of support, not just the ones in my town.

I decided to write an article about my work to submit to a magazine. But I quickly realized that I had so much information to share that I was writing the introduction to a book instead of an article. I decided to carry on and get it done quickly. Three months later, my book "Alcohol and You" was selling on major online platforms, and readers were writing reviews about how life-changing they had found it. And it was life-changing for me also, as it became a bestseller on Amazon and launched my career as a writer.

If I had delayed, if I had thought, "I'll start when I have more time", I would probably never have written the book. The voice of my Inner Critic would have had a chance to plant doubt in my mind. It would have said things like: "Who do you think you are? Are you sure you're qualified enough? Perhaps you should do another five years of research? Why do you think you can write?" And so on.

But because I got on with it immediately, my voice of self-doubt got trampled as I ran down The Path to my goal.

Here's another example: A few years ago, my wife, Antonia, was very unhappy in her job in teaching. She was working ridiculously long hours, had a long commute to her school, she was coming home late, exhausted and with work she still needed to do at home. Her doctor diagnosed her with stress. Something had to change. It would have seemed sensible for her to start applying for other jobs, but it could have taken months to organize a suitable new post. She couldn't wait. Her happiness and health were on the line.

She quit her job, with no other job to go to. At this point, her Inner Critic could have gone crazy, beating her up for doing something so reckless. But it didn't have time, as she took immediate action.

Antonia had always loved animals. Where we lived at the time was in the countryside. Our garden backed onto hundreds of acres of quiet country lanes and fields. She loved nothing more than taking our dog on long walks, as it was perfect dog-walking country. She announced she was going to start a business looking after dogs.

Right away, she started putting out adverts on cheap or free web sites and social media. I designed a small, business web site for her. She bought business insurance. The phone started ringing. She had momentum. Within a few days, she was in business and the dogs started arriving. In her first month, she earned as much as she had been earning as a teacher, doing something she loved.

The important thing to grasp is that change happened on the very first day. That's why this book is called Change Your Life Today.

But what happens after the initial rush of momentum slows? How do you keep going when self-doubt starts to creep back? How do you keep going on the bad days?

Let's look at that next.

Motivation on Demand

The concept of using The Path and taking your Daily Action makes it easy to overcome procrastination and feeling overwhelmed by your goals.

Using this valuable strategy for changing your life, most days you are likely to find that taking your Daily Action is not difficult, just so long as you are on a Path that is aligned with your deepest desire.

But even so, some days it can still feel almost impossible to get motivated. This is usually because the voice of your Inner Critic starts trying to stop you from changing. Change scares the voice, and it kicks up a fuss. That's when you need to be able to access motivation on demand because the voice has a powerful ally: familiarity.

In my professional life, I have found that familiarity is a formidable foe for clients who want to change. Familiarity leads to repetition in your daily life and hardwires our brains to adopt routines. In some ways this is useful. Having a positive daily routine is a powerful tool for getting things done, leaving time in your life for leisure. But negative routines get hardwired as well.

If you have started a fitness program, for instance, the voice will try its hardest to persuade you that the tiny twinge you just felt in your leg is a great reason to cancel your visit to the gym and get pizza delivered instead – just like you used to.

If you have given up smoking but associate having a cigarette with drinking coffee, then you risk relapsing with every cappuccino because your brain has hardwired the connection between coffee and nicotine through repetition.

So, we need a reliable way to call on motivation whenever we need it to overcome the allure of the familiar.

Motivation is misunderstood. People think getting motivated is arduous. I know I did when I was young. Procrastination seemed like the only thing I was good at. I thought I must have been born the laziest person on the planet. But I can see now that wasn't true because if something came into view that inspired me, I could be as motivated as anyone. However, I ran into difficulties when I needed the motivation to get things done which bored me. I thought I struggled to get motivated. I thought that it was something I lacked. Other people had it because they were born with it, but I had been born with a shortage.

However, as it turned out, that wasn't true.

What I didn't understand back then was that motivation is rather simple. It only requires a small movement. Think of rolling a ball down a hill. You only need a small amount of energy to get the ball moving, then momentum will take over and, in no time at all, the ball is heading downhill at speed.

And that's the trick to understanding motivation. You don't need to make gigantic efforts or get wildly hyped up. You just need to take a little action to get something going so that momentum can kick in. Momentum moves things on and creates its own energy, like the ball rolling down the hill.

Take another analogy. Imagine you are going to start your car. Do you heave it out of the garage and start pushing it down the road? No, of course not – you simply turn the key in the ignition. That's not a difficult thing to do, but it sets off a chain of events in the engine, and then you're on your way down the street.

Turning the key was like providing the motivation to start something. All you did was take the tiny action of turning the key and, moments later, half a ton of metal was on the move.

Motivation is a trick, a knack, a little technique. You just take the smallest action, and then momentum provides the energy to keep things going.

Here's a simple motivational technique that I have recommended to my clients with great success, and it works for me to keep me on my Path when I'm wavering: Taking an Easy Action Right Now.

This involves just taking a small, easy action, such as thinking: "I'll just get ready, then see how I feel."

So, if it's my day to go for a run, and the internal dialogue in my head is trying to persuade me to stay home where it's cozy, I'll think: "Oh, I'll just get my running gear on and then decide." Putting my running shoes on is easy. I can't remember a time when I've got ready and then not gone for a run. I think: "Well, I'll just do it anyway." No iron willpower is required. And by the time the voice in my head has realized what's going on, I'm half a mile down the road.

If I've had a busy day, but I still have client notes to type up, while the voice in my head is trying to persuade me to leave it until the morning, I'll think, "I'll just make a start. I can always save it later." Of course, I will carry on and finish the task, and be pleased with myself that I did it when I come into work to a clean start the next day.

So if, for example, you can't decide whether to go into town to your therapy meeting or stay home, try thinking: "I'll just get in the car and then decide." Or if you are a salesperson out on the road, and you know you should go back to the office and make five calls, but the voice is telling you to sneak home early, you could think: "Well, I'll just drop by the office and then decide."

If you don't feel in the mood to do the yoga practice you have scheduled, just try thinking: "Well, I'll go stand on my yoga mat and then decide." Then you might think: "While I'm here, I'll just do a few stretches." Before you know it, you've done your practice.

You just turned the key in the ignition of your motivational engine.

If I'm working with a client on motivation, we'll start by working out when it is that they need to use this technique. We do this by identifying when their habitual moments of self-sabotage are – the times when the inner voice gets its way. What we then do is work out a go-to action to use at that time that fits the "Easy Action Right Now" scenario. That way, you don't even need any thinking time – you just do it.

Open-Minded Outcomes

You need to be clear about the goal you are setting for yourself: the place you want to be when you reach the end of your Path. But it's worth being flexible about what the outcome will look like when you get there. That might initially seem a little contrary because we are used to being advised that we should set a goal and go for it. Indeed, the concept of The Path might seem to re-enforce that view. But it isn't a rigid philosophy.

After you have set your goal, the focus then becomes the Daily Action. You can trust that if you take this step, don't move off your Path, keep being totally honest and checking where your feet are, you will reach the end of The Path. No other outcome is possible.

But the Path is an adaptable concept. Between you deciding what your goal is and reaching that goal, many seemingly random events that you cannot currently foresee will occur. New information will come to light that you are presently unaware of.

This is a good thing because, if you are open-minded, you might have the opportunity to achieve an outcome that is even better than the one you had originally intended. I can think of many times in my life when following a Path has led me to an outcome I hadn't imagined at the outset, but which was much better than I had expected. When that happens, you realize that instigating change is exciting and enriching. Here are some examples:

I know how long I want this book to be. But by being open-minded about what I am doing, new ideas might come to me along the way that allow me to write a longer but better book.

A person who is quitting the drink for January might think it's rather cool and end up quitting for the whole year.

The dieter eating healthy food to lose weight might get the taste for it, make the change permanent, and live a longer, fitter life as a result.

Here's a true story to illustrate this further:

I once received an email out of the blue, inviting me to go to Portugal on a business trip. I was busy and I had never been interested in going to Portugal, so I could have very easily been closed-minded about the outcome and sent a polite "thanks-but-no-thanks" email back. But I was curious. All I knew about Portugal was that it was the little country next to Spain, and I was shocked at my ignorance. So, I decided to go and take a look with an open mind. I booked a flight to Lisbon.

I discovered when I got to Portugal that I loved being there – so much so that I stayed for 7 years.

As a write these words, I am back again. By being flexible about my outcomes, I have enriched my life and experienced a country and culture that had never been in my plans, but I'm really glad my Path led me there.

Another example is my writing. I described in an earlier chapter how I once wrote an article about my therapeutic work. That article grew into a book that became a bestseller. Since then, I have continued on this Path, writing more books. Now, I have a publishing company and am massively grateful to be able to share my work on a global platform. It has greatly expanded my life experience and, I hope in doing so, I have helped improve the lives of tens of thousands of readers. And all has been possible because I was open-minded about the outcome of that original article.

When I make a goal for a new project nowadays, I am always open about the outcome. I regard setting the goal as a statement of intent, and indeed, that might well be exactly where I end up at the end of that particular Path. But I'm always open to the idea that the Path might take me to an even better outcome.

This might sound a little mystic, but it's nothing of the kind. When you take your Daily Action, you will set off a chain-reaction of events. This is simply cause-and-effect in action. But where that chain of events leads you can be surprising because, all around you every day, change is happening, so you can take the same action on two consecutive days, but the result might vary.

This is how you can find success and happiness in our random world.

Recording the Stats

If you go into a sales office at, say, a motor dealer, insurance, or office equipment company, in all probability you will see a board on the wall showing the sales of the individual salespeople. The reason for this is clear. Simply seeing the numbers is motivating. If you are at the top of the sales league, you want to stay there. If you are in the middle, you want to get to the top. If you are at the bottom, you will desperately want to move up. The sales management knows this, which is why the board is there.

You can use this simple technique to help yourself along your Path. It can be applied to most things we do. There is always a way of recording the stats.

When I gave up smoking, I put up a monthly planner on the wall of the kitchen, where I couldn't help but see it many times per day. At the end of every day when I hadn't smoked, I would put a sticker on that date. I made getting to the end of the day and putting my sticker on the chart the most important thing in my life for a month because I knew how beneficial stopping smoking would be. My goal was to reach the end of that month with a sticker on my chart every day. I was simply recording the number of days, one by one, in a very graphic way.

Does this sound too simple? Surely there must be more to it than that? Well, I had already tried more complicated ways. I had spent a fortune on nicotine replacement products, and a couple of years smothered in nicotine patches. I had forced myself to chew that vile-tasting nicotine gum. I had used nicotine inhalers. I had read Alan Carr's book, which told me that I could stop smoking "the easy way". Did it work? No, it didn't make the slightest difference. I'm sure it has worked for many people, but for me, there was no "easy way".

But there was a simple way. Simple and easy don't mean the same thing, as I would discover. But I found the way.

I had a Path: to get to the end of the month. I had a Daily Action: to be able to put my no-smoking sticker up at the end of the day. I had the monthly planner as motivation. I was recording the stats.

All my previous attempts to stop smoking had ended in total failure – and I had made countless attempts. But this simple method worked the first time.

If you have ever been addicted to nicotine, as I had been for decades, you will know just how difficult giving up is. Research shows that 40% of smokers try to give up every year, yet the number of smokers only comes down by 1% per year. That means there is a huge failure rate. I can understand why.

Nicotine withdrawal is horrible. Your head is spinning for days, you cannot concentrate, and you have cravings hitting you all the time. I was even hallucinating on the first couple of days of giving up. But this uncomplicated method got me through to the end of the month. Then I knew there was no going back. It had been so painful, there was no way I was ever going to endure that again. I haven't smoked at all since.

Another example of the power of recording the stats happened only yesterday. I have an app on my phone that records the number of paces I take every day. It's a great little app. It can tell the difference between when I'm running or walking, it tells me how far I have gone, and it tells me how many calories I have burned.

But the most important stat for me is simply the total number of paces. I set myself a minimum daily target of 8,000 paces. I can go over the minimum as much as I like, but I have made a deal with myself that I will do that minimum every day. It's non-negotiable. Whatever is going on that day, however busy I am, or whatever the weather is like, I will find a way to reach that minimum.

Yesterday, when I got home late afternoon, I checked my app and realized that I was about a thousand steps short of the minimum. That immediately motivated me. I didn't need to stop and think. I went straight out again. I took a brisk walk down to my local beach and explored part of it I don't usually go on. It was fun. By going after those steps, I had enhanced my day. In the end, I was a couple of thousand steps over my minimum. But if I hadn't been keeping the stats on my app, I probably would have just sat down at home and turned on the computer.

Another use I have found for that particular app is in helping me sleep. I have a recurring problem with sleeping. I can get to sleep easily enough. The problem is that I will wake up in the night, my mind will be busy and I find it difficult to get back to sleep. I tried various remedies. The pharmacy recommended an antihistamine-based pill, but that didn't help me sleep and I felt woozy in the morning. My doctor prescribed me low-dosage Amitriptyline, which did help me sleep, but turned me into a drooling zombie in the morning. I tried listening to relaxing downloads at bedtime, but no result there either. I tried various recommendations for sleep hygiene, but again no luck. I also experimented with what I ate or drank to see if that make a difference. I couldn't find any.

But then I started analyzing the data from my walking app. I realized there seemed to be a direct connection between the distance I had walked during the day and having a good night's sleep. It had to be brisk walking or running. The magic number I came up with was four miles. If I briskly walked four miles in the day, I would probably sleep well. Four miles for me is about 8,000 paces, which is why I have put that in my app as my daily minimum.

Curiously, that four miles figure seems quite exact for me: it's the sweet spot I need to hit. If I fall short by just half a mile, I will probably be awake in the night. If I walk a longer distance, I don't sleep any longer. I don't have a problem with motivation to do my four miles as I know I won't sleep if I miss my target. Of course, there are all sorts of other health benefits in walking that distance every day, so come what may, I need to make time for it.

I also use an app currently to record what I eat to ensure that I have eaten enough high-nutrient foods every day. I have realized that this is also where I need to record the stats. It is easy to read up on a subject like nutrition and think, "Yes, I'll do that. I'll eat all that good stuff." But then you go and get on with your busy day, and you simply forget. But not if you are keeping a record. What's more, it's satisfying at the end of the day to see my record of all the good stuff I have eaten.

I had a manager once who had a saying: "What gets recorded gets done." He used to annoy me with that phrase and all the ways he made me record what I was doing. I got resentful. Surely he could trust me to get on with my job. But my productivity went up. I got more done. The quality of my work got better. I have to admit he was right.

Your Cheerleaders

One of my favorite quotations is "You begin by always expecting good things to happen." That comes from a book by Tom Hopkins, who you might be familiar with if you work in sales, as Hopkins is a legend in the world of sales training.

When I was in my twenties, before I trained as a counselor, I got into sales work. The reason was money. With my first child on the way, I needed to earn more, and sales seemed to be the way that I could. I wasn't very good at it. That's not surprising. Doing something just for the money is rarely a happy arrangement because it isn't your true desire. But I needed the stuff.

Then I discovered a book called *How to Master the Art of Selling* by Tom Hopkins. I don't think I ever really mastered the art of selling as it wasn't my calling – but I got a lot better. As I remember, the book had lots of handy sales techniques. But what sticks with me now, three decades later, is the bit that changed my life.

Hopkins talks in his book about a character called Jack Bumyears. This is the person hanging around the office who is a perennial underachiever. He hates seeing new people coming in and doing well because they show up his own shortcomings. He is the person who won't take on new ideas. He is the person who gossips behind people's backs and likes to talk everything down. He is the voice of negativity that drains the enthusiasm and joy out of those around him.

So why did Jack Bumyears change my life? Well, two reasons:

Firstly, after reading that book, if I ever find myself being negative and talking things down, I will think: "Oh no, I'm being like Jack Bumyears," and that will snap me out of it.

Secondly, it alerted me to all the Bumyears-like people in my life. We all have them. If you are totally honest, you will probably admit that you go into Bumyears-mode from time to time yourself. We are all prone to griping and moaning sometimes.

But plenty of people live in a world of fault-finding and complaining. Indeed, some people seem to need it, like it is their default setting to seek out the worst in any situation.

For such people, social media must have been like a gift from Heaven. Do you belong to any groups on Facebook or other platforms? I do, as they have their uses. I am on groups for authors and also for ex-pats in Portugal, for instance. Being able to share information with like-minded people can be valuable. But some people seem to be on these groups just to be sarcastic and nasty, while hiding behind the anonymity of a profile page.

Just recently I saw a post on an ex-pat group from a lady who lived in a remote area, wanting to know where she could source some ingredients for cake-making. Not a contentious post, you would think. But no. The trolls were out making snide comments accompanied by laughing emojis. The thread was long, and when you scanned down towards the end, people were having the social media equivalent of fisticuffs with each other over politics. Cake making had been forgotten and the post was being used as an excuse to vent hate for people with different views. Unbelievable, but sadly true.

People like this are just a drain on your mental and emotional resources, whether you encounter them in your home environment, at work, or online. They have a knack for being able to wake up the voice of self-doubt in your head and generally make you feel that life is a drudge.

So, what can you do?

Well, you can start by setting an example and not behaving like a Bumyears yourself. You can also do your best to avoid such people. But this is not always easy. Online, you can just block someone, but if the Bumyears in your life is a close member of your family or your boss, that's a different matter. Realistically, you can't purge your life of every Bumyears – they are everywhere. Even inside the best of us, a Bumyears is trying to get out.

What you can do, however, is to counter all this negativity with your supporters. Who agrees with what you are trying to do? Who would offer you words of encouragement on a challenging day? Who would love to cheer you onwards across the finishing line of your Path? These are the people you would be wise to hang out with, whether it be people in your day-to-day life or online. These are the people who will help you find success and happiness.

I think it is a good exercise to take a sheet of paper and brainstorm with yourself exactly who these people are. Some will be obvious – if you have a supportive partner or parent, for example. Others might be less obvious. Maybe a cheerful person at the front desk at work, or someone who shares a particular interest with you.

When you consciously recognize who these wonderful people are, you can cultivate your relationship with them, and they are there for you to tap into when the forces of negativity are trying to sap your strength.

Next, it's time to look at the super-powerful strategy of Achievement Stacking.

Achievement Stacking

You read earlier about how Antonia started her dog care business and achieved immediate success. She didn't wait until she was ready, she just went for it, and it worked right away.

Her success continued. She was getting plenty of work. Her marketing costs were virtually zero. The phone was ringing. She was even being able to pick and choose which dogs she took on. The owners were happy. Some were becoming regular customers, which is what any business wants: repeat business. They had confidence in Antonia. She was clearly doing a great job. This was not surprising as she was very organized and had previous experience of working with dogs from being a volunteer in an animal rescue center. She was insured and had taken an animal first aid course. She was prepared. She had faith in her ability.

But, despite her obvious ability to run her business, a curious thing happened. About eight weeks into the business, she had bookings and money coming in fast. Yet, she started to worry that someone would challenge her and say things like: "Who do you think you are? What right have you to run a business like this?"

It seemed she had an attack of Impostor Syndrome. This is where self-doubt leads someone to feel they could get exposed as a fraud, despite obvious evidence to the contrary. It's a tactic that your Inner Critic loves to exploit to halt your desire for change.

Ironically, Impostor Syndrome is often a sign that things are going right. It follows an achievement. For example, someone who lands their dream job might find that they feel in over their head, that they aren't up to the work, and aren't equal to their peers, even though there is no evidence to support that view.

In Antonia's case, that little voice of her Inner Critic, which had been swept aside by her initial burst of activity and success, had time to recover and was starting to undermine her. It could have led her away from her Path.

These attacks of self-doubt have no logic. I have experienced it many times. In my work, I have run hundreds of therapeutic groups in outpatient services. This is where I have around 20 people who are in treatment come in for a structured discussion, led by me and usually another colleague, on a certain topic.

I have a good reputation among my colleagues for facilitating these groups – it's one of my strengths. I usually feel totally comfortable, like I'm in my natural environment. Yet sometimes, for no reason, I will see the room filling up with clients and suddenly start feeling that I'm not up to the job today. I will feel like a fraud. The feeling usually goes as soon as the group starts and I get into my stride. But it's unsettling.

I helped one client who had previously been in the military, and during that time, he had flown thousands of miles and made dozens of parachute jumps. Then one day after he left the military, he was flying home from a vacation on a short-haul flight. With no warning, he felt himself breathing erratically and sweating. He felt light-headed and frightened. Out of nowhere, he suddenly developed a fear of flying. He was unable to fly for years afterwards.

Confidence comes and goes with us all. Fear can come and tap you on the shoulder at the most inconvenient times, and you can be sure it will happen often while you are changing your life for the better. So how do you find confidence when you need it?

If you are using The Path, try reminding yourself that as long as you do your Daily Action and don't allow yourself to be dragged off The Path, you will reach your goal – no other outcome is possible. Repeat this to yourself as often as you like.

But if self-doubt still troubles you, try a technique I have successfully used many times with clients and also myself. I call it Achievement Stacking. There are two variants I use: the lifetime version and the daily version.

We'll start with the lifetime version, which you do only once. Take a notebook. Then, think about your life so far. Think about its different aspects and give them different category names. What you choose is up to you – it's your life – but for instance you might choose: Childhood, School, College, Relationships, Work, Parenting, Helping Others, Playing Sports, and so on.

Now, for each part of your life, I want you to think of achievements you have made and, for each category, make a vertical list, starting at the bottom of the page and moving up a line each time write down an achievement. This is your stack. Make your stack as high as you can.

Think of ten categories in your life, and then keep digging down into your memory for each category until you have a stack of at least ten achievements for each category. You are aiming for a hundred in total.

Does a hundred sound too many? No, it isn't. This is a lifetime inventory of your achievements you are creating. You will have to tailor it to yourself because, if you are sixty years old, you will naturally have a lot more material to work with than someone who is twenty.

Certain categories will be easier for some people than others. If you did well at school and went on to do a degree, then getting a high stack for Education will be a breeze. If you dropped out of school, it will be more difficult. But don't give up. If you dig down, you will find those achievements.

What you call an achievement will also be personal to you. What is routine to one person, would be an achievement to another. Most of us wouldn't regard buying the groceries as an achievement. But for someone who is trying to overcome chronic agoraphobia, going out to buy a can of beans would be a genuine achievement.

If you are career-oriented, then you might break down the work category into several sub-categories, whereas someone focused on bringing up a family might sub-categorize parenting. If I were doing this exercise, I would think of the names of clients whose lives I feel I have impacted for the better, then turn that into a stack. I might also list all the training courses I have completed for another stack. These would be tall stacks and I would be up to 100 in no time.

If you are struggling, when you have identified one achievement in a particular stack, try asking yourself "What else?" Keep asking yourself "What else?" until you are sure you've built up that stack as high as you can.

I have had clients whose lives were highly challenged look at me in disbelief when I asked them to do an Achievement Stack. People have said things like "You must be joking. My life is a mess, and I've never achieved anything!" But once they have made a start and kept asking "What else?" they have amazed themselves with what they have achieved.

Remember, this is a big inventory. Take your time. Do it over a few days, as old achievements will start popping up in your head that your conscious mind had forgotten about. Enjoy the process. This is all about you.

When you feel sure that you have completed the inventory and can look with satisfaction at many tall stacks in your notebook, keep it somewhere safe. Every time you feel self-doubt creeping in, look at your stacks. Take heart from your past achievements.

You might like to highlight the ten or twenty achievements that give you the most satisfaction. Perhaps keep them on a note on your phone so you can refer to them and take strength from them any time you're feeling challenged or unsure of yourself.

You might like to recite them to yourself every morning when you wake up, or when you take the dog for a walk. It's a great way to build self-belief. If you have achieved all these things in the past, then surely taking your Daily Action along your Path is easy.

The above version of Achievement Stacking is a one-off tactic. The shorter version will help maintain self-belief daily. This is how it works.

At the end of the day, take a couple of minutes to think about your day. Pick out your achievements that day. These are likely to be much smaller things than on your lifetime achievement inventory. They are things that if you hadn't done this exercise, you might have forgotten about.

It could be a telephone conversation where you have said something that helped a client or a friend. It could be an email you wrote that you thought communicated a point particularly well. It could have been an act of kindness to your partner. Maybe you had to be especially patient with your child. You might have faced up to making a call you had been putting off to an authority figure. You filed your tax return. Or maybe you just made a great sandwich for lunch.

Create your stack for the day. Some days it will be easy. But where you might find it really helpful is on a bad day. You know the sort of day. It's the day your boss gives you a hard time for no obvious reason. You get a parking ticket. You have a huge bust-up with your partner. You dent your car. Dinner is a disaster. Your head feels like a sack of worries, and your stomach is churning like a washing machine.

On days like these, it's difficult to find the achievements – but all the more reason to look hard for them. Even if they are just small, find at least three. It will give you faith that even when things seem to be going badly, there are still good things going on. And if you have done your Daily Action, you will still be on The Path to your goal.

At the end of your week, take a look at your daily stacks from the week. Pick out your favorites. Take a few moments to enjoy again some satisfaction from your achievements. It will give you the momentum to do more next week.

When you have finished your Achievement Stacks, it's time to move up a level. It's time to look at Super Empowerment.

Super Empowerment

Stephanie was a well presented, articulate woman in her thirties who regularly attended one of my therapeutic groups. The group was themed around self-management. The format was that I would begin by asking the participants if they had any current life issues they would like to discuss with the group, and from that, I would draw up an agenda for discussion.

Stephanie always wanted to discuss her mother. They had a volatile relationship. She would frequently be in tears about something her mother had said. It sounded like her mother was very judgmental and had a way of saying things that really hit Stephanie's weak spots.

Stephanie's story was that she had regular rage-attacks, which were invariably triggered by an argument with her mother. She didn't normally drink, but on these occasions, she would hit the vodka and completely go off the rails. She would become uncontrollable; she would break up the house, and give a verbal mauling to anyone who got in her way. It had all got too much for her husband, Mike, who had moved out and taken the children with him.

Not surprisingly, members of the group suggested she should attend anger management, but Stephanie would not. "It's not me that's the problem, it's my mother. She's the one who needs treatment, not me," she insisted.

Then one week, she came to the group, her eyes puffed up and red, in floods of tears. She had had another outburst of rage. She wanted to talk to me alone, so one of my colleagues took the group, while I made Stephanie some tea, and then we talked.

"It was my mother again. She says it's just as well Mike's got the kids, she says I'm not fit to be a mother". Remarks like that hurt Stephanie the most. Not being under the same roof as her children was an open wound which, for some reason, her mother couldn't resist poking.

"I went home, but I bought some vodka on the way. Then I started messaging people. I was so upset. My best friend came over to try to help," she said. "But I just totally lost it. I was so angry. I thought she was just trying to interfere and I got really abusive. She won't speak to me now. I'm so sorry. I don't know what came over me. I've lost my husband. My kids aren't speaking to me. Now I've lost my best friend. And it's all my mother's fault. What can I do about her?"

"You may not be able to do anything about her," I said. "You can't change her, and you don't have power over the horrible things that she says. But you can change the way you react to her. You actually have the power to stop these events that are causing you pain."

We discussed that as long as she reacted instinctively to her mother's jibes, she would be her mother's victim. But if she took responsibility for how she reacted and accepted some anger management training, she could stop her rage-attacks, and that would turn her from being a victim to being empowered.

"That's not fair. It's her that should get treatment, not me", she reiterated.

"I see your point," I said, "and I understand why you think it's unfair. But it's not a question of whether it's fair or not. It's about you moving the power in your relationship from her to you. It's about stopping you damaging your own interests. It's about you getting the life that you want. It's about you being empowered."

As children, we learn to shift the blame onto others. How many times have you heard children exclaiming something like, "It was her fault, not mine." Children will deny their actions, even when it's blatantly untrue. But they will do it with such passion that they will believe it's true.

As adults, most of us do the same. It becomes our go-to response to blame anyone else but ourselves for things that go wrong in our lives. And we do it with such a passion that we believe it ourselves. It's what's often referred to as being in denial, and it comes from the reflex to blame others.

But while it might feel good to blame someone else, you are in fact making a victim of yourself. You are effectively saying that your happiness and security are in the hands of other people. That's asking for trouble, because you have no power over other people, yet you have handed all the power to them. If they let you down – which they probably will, even if unintentionally - you are the one who suffers, and you blame them to vent your frustration.

In the end, Stephanie did accept help. She learnt some techniques to control her reactions to her mother. She learnt to call a counselling service rather than reach for the vodka – she could let off steam safely on the phone to a counsellor and diffuse the situation. Having an outlet for her feelings was vital. Feelings of outrage and injustice are exceptionally painful and can blow a massive hole through your ability to think rationally. Having a safe way to vent those feelings is much more sensible than just trying to bottle them up, as that risks an even bigger explosion at a later point.

Stephanie worked at her reactions and it paid off. She came to understand that if she waited for her mother to change her ways, she could wait forever. But she had the power to change her side of the relationship immediately. No one got hurt anymore, especially Stephanie herself. She still thought it was unfair, but the benefits of gaining control of her life outweighed the feeling of resentment. Her friend forgave her.

The last time I saw her, her children were talking to her and she was hoping Mike would move back in with her.

Another client, Gwenda, was dependent on social media. Every time I saw her in the waiting room before a group workshop, she was on Facebook or some other site on her phone. Even during the group sessions,

I could see her taking sneaky looks at her phone.

Her moods would swing dramatically and were dependant on the reactions she got to her posts. Her happiness was in the hands of other people, many of them strangers she had never met, but with whom she was "friends". People can be cruel on social media, and one harsh word would bring Gwenda's world crashing down. They were not being fair, she said. They had misunderstood what she meant. There were often tears.

For most people, it is human nature to want to be liked. But Gwenda had an addiction to approval, and it made her unhappy. She could have a dozen people saying nice things about her, but if there was one disapproving comment, she would focus on that, and ignore all the nice stuff. And it wasn't just social media. In a group, she was always fishing for compliments, and you could see her expression drop if she didn't get them.

It took Gwenda a long time to grasp that she had made herself a victim and that the power to change that was in her hands. As far as social media was concerned, she could simply turn it off, take the apps off her phone, and it was gone, just like that, in an instant. But she couldn't just turn off meeting people face-to-face. We worked on this, and she started to understand that the problem wasn't other people's reactions, it was her expectations.

Gwenda would expect people, often strangers, to react positively to her. But there was no basis for her expectations. Other people could not live up to Gwenda's expectations, because they had no idea what her expectations were. She had not communicated her expectations to them and they weren't mind-readers. Gwenda was being illogical. But she was also being very human.

Once Gwenda realized that her expectations of other people came from her being judgmental of how other people should behave, she could start to let go and take responsibility for her own thinking. It was that word "should" causing trouble again.

Taking responsibility for what happens to you is genuinely life-changing. You can try it yourself now. Is there an area of your life where you feel outraged by someone else's behaviour? If you can put aside your emotion, can you see a way you can take control by managing your reactions?

You need to be really honest with yourself. Remember that Path is an acronym of Planning and Total Honesty. Without honesty, you might fall off your Path and never reach your goal.

It might feel unfair. It might feel that the other person should behave differently. But rather than be resentful, which will only make you unhappy, try to get some acceptance that they are just like that, you can't change them, and you have a part to play in what's happened yourself.

It is not totally their fault.

Acceptance doesn't mean you have lost. Acceptance is not the same as resignation. Acceptance is a jumping off point to something better. Once you have acceptance, you can then take action to change your reactions to what whatever is happening. And that will allow you to breathe easier and allow some contentment to come into your life.

Another benefit of changing how you react is that it might encourage the other person to behave better towards you. We tend to get our own behaviour reflected back to us. To take a simple example, if you approach someone you are about to meet for the first time with a smile, it's likely you will get a smile back. But if you have a face like thunder, it's unlikely you will get a smile.

I can't guarantee that the person who has been causing you pain will change to reflect your behaviour. Some people are so self-absorbed they don't notice. But it's worth a shot, you don't know until you try.

You might like to take a little time to reflect on this chapter. My clients who have absorbed this concept have found it deeply life-changing; I know it was for me.

Then, when you are ready, let's move on and discover the magic of living life with a lighter touch.

Living with A Lighter Touch

A few years ago, Antonia and I decided on a life change. We were living in a house in the idyllic county of Dorset in England. Dorset is a place of outrageously stunning villages, with thatched-roofed cottages, rolling hillsides, and a spectacular coastline – the sort of place the English Tourist Board might put on the cover of its brochure. It would be many people's dream to live somewhere like that, and we were living the dream.

But it didn't feel like a happy dream. We like to be outdoors a lot and, frankly, the weather in England is pretty dreary for six or seven months of the year. Also, we were working in demanding, stressful jobs just to pay for the mortgage, bills, and vacations.

I was working in an outpatient unit. Being a counselor probably might sound easy. You might imagine clients turning up on time, ready for their weekly chat. It all sounds rather cozy. But the reality of working with people who are often in crisis is not like that at all. It can be seriously demanding, with clients pitching up on the doorstep in all states of distress.

At the same time, Antonia was working in a special unit for children with severe emotional disorders, often working long shifts and anti-social hours. We were taking three or four vacations a year to warm, sunny places just to keep a feeling of balance in our lives.

We realized we had dug ourselves into a stressful hole. It can happen to anyone. You are so busy day-to-day that you don't realize that you are digging until one day you look up and suddenly see how deep you have got yourself in. We needed change, and we knew it was up to us to instigate that change. Simply wishing for something better wouldn't work. We needed to take action.

We started by taking stock of where we were. Our lives were full, and we needed to clear the decks to be able to start making changes. Changing your life becomes more difficult if unnecessary commitments and possessions are weighing you down, and we had got ourselves into that position.

It's so easy to fill your life with clutter, both physical and mental. It's easy to overburden yourself with commitments that you don't need any more, and possessions that are doing nothing for you.

We all need to accept some commitments, but few of them are life-long. And life isn't about having a house full of miscellaneous stuff. You can have possessions that are like a weight tied around your neck, or you can use possessions to facilitate your happiness, and when they have served their purpose, you can let them go and move on. Possessions can be short-term, like a hire car or a hotel room. You don't need permanent ownership to get pleasure from them – just a temporary lease on their time.

It was on one of our vacations that we began to take stock. We had returned to Portugal's sunny Algarve region for a visit. In the past, we had lived there for seven years but hadn't been back for almost as long. It felt strange going back. I wasn't sure how I would react. But I needn't have been concerned. It immediately felt like home. On the first night, we decided we wanted to return there to live, if not all the time, then at least during the months that are wet and gloomy in England.

It sounded like a great idea: live in a gorgeous part of England in the summer, and then Portugal the rest of the year. But how could we achieve this? Surely, we would need to be rich to do that? How about our jobs? Surely, we would have to take on even greater financial commitments and the stress that comes with that? How about all our possessions?

We had our goal, but we needed a plan so that The Path would reveal itself.

And it did.

We called it *living with a lighter touch*.

Rather than take on more expense and commitments to realize our dream of a two-center lifestyle, we decided to go the opposite way: we would cut our commitments and outgoings, be able to save money, be happier, stop working so hard, and live a life that was a dream.

Sounds impossible? We've done it. Here's how:

We looked at our situation. We lived in a family house, but there were only two of us and the dog. The youngest of our children had left home. We only regularly used about half the house. We didn't need all the space. So why were we living there? Why were we working ourselves into the ground to pay for it?

The rest of the house, the half we didn't use, was only useful as somewhere to keep all our possessions. But why did we have all this stuff? Most of it we didn't need. I mean, why did we have hundreds of CDs that we had acquired over decades when we didn't play them anymore? So, we turned the ones we liked into mp3s, which we store on a cloud somewhere, and got rid of all the discs.

All the books we never read went as well. We can store hundreds of books on a reading device and then just have a small bookshelf for the ones we wanted to keep in print format.

Antonia had a lot of items of sentimental value, but she realized that most of them she rarely looked at, so she took photos of them so that she could remind herself of the sentiment and let the physical objects go.

I went through my wardrobe. About half the clothes in there had been unused for at least a year. I was keeping clothes on the basis that I might wear them one day, but if that day hadn't come in over a year, it probably was never going to arrive, so half my wardrobe went to charity.

I found it hard to part with my fly-fishing gear. I had a bond with it. But as I hadn't fished in six years, there was no reason to keep it. It was just taking up space in a storage room. So, I closed my eyes and let it go one morning at a car boot sale.

Then the furniture started to go. Why did we have three sets of tables and chairs just for us two? We never watched the television, so we gave it to someone who was grateful for it. Gradually the house started to empty.

Over the next few months, we sold what we could on websites like Gumtree. We were frequent visitors to car boot sales. The local charity shops started to bulge with all our donated items.

The point of all this was so we could downsize. I had worked out how much all those vacations had been costing us. We had been spending a lot of money just so we could spend about 30 days of the year in sunny places and recharge ourselves.

I ran a calculator over how much we had been spending and compared it to what we would be spending in our ideal new lifestyle. The figures were amazing.

If we downsized and had a smaller place as our summer home in England, we would no longer need a mortgage. Then we could rent an apartment on the Algarve coast of Portugal for eight months of the year, which would cost less than the vacations had been costing us.

We would no longer need vacations, as we would be living in a sunny place. At the same time, we would feel the relief of having fewer commitments, and be less stressed and happier. And our wonderful new lifestyle would cost us less than our stressful lifestyle.

Brilliant!

There was just one snag. We would still need income while we were in Portugal. We would still need to work. But we didn't want to put ourselves in the situation where we were working all hours in Portugal, find ourselves back under pressure, and lose the benefits of having a good lifestyle.

But I believe that if The Path you are on is the right one for you, solutions will appear. There are always going to be obstructions in your way, but on the correct Path, getting past these will feel like opening doors, not like breaking through brick walls – it will flow. As long as you continue to take action, you will reach your goal.

When my first book became a success, I realized the potential of using my professional training in another way. I now had an alternative to being employed. I could publish some more of my writing and free myself up from the need to be in one location all the time.

As for Antonia's work, she found a job that was ideal for her at an English-speaking school in Portugal. So that she wouldn't have the daily grind of commuting, we found an apartment in a seaside town 10 minutes from her work, with a sea view, beach, and palm trees included. Then, during the school's summer break, we could enjoy the summer in England.

We transformed our lives by taking Daily Actions over a period of time until eventually we found ourselves at the end of our Path and living our dream. No mysticism, no so-called Law of Attraction, nor intense, motivational training courses needed. We had simply harnessed the compounding power of action leading to an outcome, repeatedly, over time.

The first time we moved to Portugal, which was 20 years ago, we arrived in two cars, which were packed to the roof with stuff we thought was essential. Then we had a container of more things we thought we couldn't leave behind delivered from England. As it turned out, most of the stuff we had delivered at great expense wasn't of much use at all. We had just moved a load of clutter across Europe.

The second time we moved to Portugal, 4 years ago, we had learned from our previous experience, and it was different. We had set ourselves the target of moving in one car, and we wouldn't get anything delivered. It sounds far too little, moving to a different country, with just a few bags in the car. But we had become ruthless at working out what we needed. What would be the point in bringing lots of kitchen equipment, for instance, when there would be equipment in the new place we would be renting? So, we just took clothes, work items like laptops, and a few personal items. There was even room for my golf clubs. We moved country in one saloon car.

Back in England, we now have a mortgage-free loft apartment to return to when we choose. The location is wonderful, with stunning views over the West Country. A management company looks after the building maintenance. The bills are low. We can just lock up and leave for as long as we like, whenever it suits us.

84

So, we are now in Portugal and plan to return to our home in England to enjoy next summer and catch up with family and friends.

Living life with a lighter touch has become fundamental to our view of the world. It means that we are not stressed. We have what we need to keep us happy and discard things when they no longer serve us.

This could mean discarding physical things like clothes or books that can go to a charity shop, where they can serve someone else. It could mean discarding our current apartment in Portugal if we decide we want to live somewhere else – which will be a simple matter as we don't own it – and then someone else will have the opportunity to enjoy it.

It means not holding on to ideas that no longer serve us. It means having the flexibility to make our lives a rolling creation. Maybe after next summer in England, we will come back to Portugal. But maybe we will go to live for a while in Spain or Italy or Florida.

We don't need to think about that now. Our next Path will reveal itself if we continue to take Daily Action and live by our beliefs and values. Action always leads to an outcome.

We have that freedom now. By downsizing what we don't need, we have a bigger life.

So, could living life with a lighter touch benefit you? True, you might not want to move around as we do. You might be happy living where you are. But are you weighed down by ideas, commitments, and possessions that no longer serve you? Do you get stressed working all hours just to pay the bills so you can keep working? Is changing your life for the better so difficult because you don't have the mental or physical space to work with? Do you spend your time doing things that you think you should do, rather than what you desire?

There are some commitments we make that we want to be permanent, such as to the people we love. These commitments are a joy, not a burden. But commitments to paying for things that don't serve you anymore, or to ideas you no longer believe in, are just clutter in your life.

You can take the first step to living with a lighter touch right now, today.

Have a look around you. What can you see that no longer serves you? What can you let go of? It may be a physical thing. It may be an attitude that keeps causing you problems. It may be a habit.

Let go of something now. When you let go of physical or mental clutter, you make space for something better. You make space for a little magic to come into your life.

One thing you might want to make space for is more success. Let's talk about that next.

Serving up Success

Before I became a full-time author, I was working in a government-funded counseling service. It so happened that I was transferred to a new location. I was unimpressed by my new place of work. It was seriously underfunded, leading to a lack of adequately qualified staff. This meant that everyone was under pressure with ridiculously heavy workloads. Staff morale had sunk so far that all the talk in the office was about leaving. Some staff were on long-term sick leave with stress. The management seemed to have lost direction and had almost given up.

The atmosphere transmitted itself to the clients, who were losing faith in the service, and numbers of engagements with the service were dropping. I wondered what on earth I had gotten myself into.

My job was to carry out clinical assessments, one-to-one counseling, and run group workshops. The workshops were a part of my job I had always enjoyed – it was great to have a roomful of people to work with. I was given two workshops per week to run at the new location. They were based on personal development. I had a dedicated meeting room to use, which could seat twenty people.

But there was a major drawback: because client numbers were dropping, I was only getting two or three clients attending, and sometimes no one turned up at all, which was dispiriting. I couldn't see myself staying in the job for long.

As luck would have it, I had a vacation booked a couple of weeks after I started at the new location, so I had an opportunity to take stock. When I arrived at my vacation location, a lovely resort in the Canary Islands, life seemed better and the sun was shining. But the thought of going back to my job hung over me like a dark cloud.

However, have you ever found that when you are looking for a solution, something that you hadn't thought about will keep cropping up until you take notice? I think what is going on is that when you have a problem, your subconscious mind starts scanning for solutions, and if it thinks it has found something, it will keep dropping hints.

In this instance, the word service kept coming to my attention. I had brought my reading device with me to use by the swimming pool, so I downloaded a couple of books and read about service. It changed my working life.

I realized that all my life up until that point, I had been thinking about work backwards. I had always looked at work in terms of what I could gain. But I needed to look instead at what I could give. How could I better serve my clients, co-workers, and employers?

The logic ran that if I focused on providing great service, then I didn't need to concern myself with how I would be rewarded because great service gets rewarded.

It's a simple enough concept. For instance, if you are a waiter and give your guests great service, you will have more fun in your job, your guests will have a more enjoyable dining experience, and also you will be the one who gets the best tips. Everyone wins. I thought a lot about how I could apply all this to my work.

I resolved that when I got back to work, I would commit to delivering great service. And I did. I didn't wait until I was ready – I threw myself into it from the moment I walked through the door on my return to work. I felt motivated and excited to apply the concept of service.

It seemed to me that the best way of making a difference quickly was through the group workshops because that was where you could engage with the largest number of people. When I started thinking in terms of what other people wanted rather than what I wanted, I realized that I needed to run workshops based on what was truly relevant to the clients, not what I thought they should hear.

So, the first thing I did when I got back to work was to move my desk from a private office to the reception area. That way, I would see all the clients when they turned up for appointments or to make enquiries, and I canvassed them about what they would like to cover in the workshops.

People got curious and started turning up for the workshops. They got engaged in the content because it was what they wanted. I just had to gently guide the discussion. I made it more interactive and fun. We had videos and quizzes. I got people moving around rather than being rooted to the chair. I brought in advisers to speak on subjects the clients had requested. I got the meeting room spruced up, looking more welcoming, and put fresh fruit out for clients to graze on and the best quality coffee we could afford. In the good weather, we ran workshops on the beach. In short, I was focused on serving my clients as best I could rather than focusing on what I could get out of the job.

It worked. The numbers attending grew rapidly. We ran out of chairs and had people standing or sitting on the floor in the meeting room, so I created extra workshops to cope with the demand. The whole place started to get a buzz about it. We attracted some new staff with a positive mindset who enjoyed the re-invented atmosphere.

We had momentum.

Word started to get around the county, and workers in other counseling facilities started got in touch. They had heard what was happening and wanted to find out more. The turnaround was huge.

I was rewarded in several ways. My job got a whole lot more fun. I had the pleasure of seeing more clients responding to treatment. I was given an improved work contract.

Moreover, serving others became my go-to. When I felt a bit low or tired, I would go and find someone to serve because if I was focused on someone else, my own little troubles would go away, and I would feel better. It's impossible to be self-absorbed and focused on someone else at the same time. You can try this yourself. If you're feeling a bit down, find someone to serve, even if in just a small way, and you will probably feel better.

Another aspect of this story is that I was trying to innovate in the way that I was serving. The interactivity of my workshops was new to the clients, who liked it and felt more engaged. I gave the workshops catchy names. I had a leaflet printed up with info on the workshops and, crucially, I didn't just write a dry description of what the workshop contained. Instead, I listed the benefits the client would get from attending to make it real and relevant for people.

Everyone who entered the building had a leaflet given to them. It sounds like a small thing, but no one had done that before. And I thanked the clients for attending. Even though they were coming to us with their troubles, they felt wanted.

So, can you use service to enhance your life and those around you? Can you better serve employers or customers? Can you even apply it to your private life? If you do, you will surely attract benefits.

Now that you know about the power of serving, let's look further at how it can pay off in your life.

Creating Something out of Nothing

I find that being able to create something out of nothing is exhilarating. It shows the power of your mind. You can look at an empty space and, armed with nothing more than your imagination and a notepad, you can design the most amazing things. Then by following a Path, you can bring it into reality.

In the early days of the Internet, I found web design amazing. I bought a book on the subject and shut myself off in a room for a month while I designed my first website. It was a travel information site that would look very basic compared with what we have today. But I put it online to see what happened.

A new-style search engine that had started to get some market share listed my site and the page visit counter started to move. In fact, it started to move quickly. That new search engine was Google. People were looking at my site and the repeat hits showed they liked it. Eventually, a big company bought my site, and I was financially rewarded for innovatively serving travelers. As the internet grew, big money moved in, and it became much more difficult to do what I had done. But I was hooked on creation.

I find it awesome to think that in just a few weeks from my writing these words today, people will be downloading the digital versions of this book from online bookstores, and the paperback version will be shipping from warehouses in the United States and Europe. Technology is awesome, and embracing it is something else that has changed my life.

In this chapter, I'm going to explore ways in which you can create and make things happen in the physical world, using just your imagination. This could be a business, charity, club, or society. It could be for profit, for the well-being of your town, for your family and friends, or simply for the fun of turning your thoughts into reality.

When I look at the creative process to bring an enterprise into being, I look for three key elements:

- Service. Who are you going to serve?
- Innovation. What can you bring to the client that makes you different?
- Specialist Knowledge. Why should anyone listen to you?

If you look at the story of my workshops in the previous chapter, you can see that it had all three of these elements. I had a specific group of clients I wanted to serve, I had innovated in how to present the workshops, and I had specialist knowledge from all my training and previous experience.

When Antonia started the dog care business we discussed earlier in the book, she knew who she wanted to serve: dog owners who wanted their pets to have personalized care. She was innovative in only ever accepting a small number of dogs at any time so that she could attend to their individual needs in a homely setting. And she had specialist knowledge, having worked with large numbers of dogs before in an animal rescue center. The business was an act of pure creation. She hadn't taken over an existing business. It was entirely the product of her imagination, and it all came into existence in a matter of days.

My first book had all the elements. I knew exactly the readers I wanted to serve: problem drinkers who wanted help. I was innovating because I knew there wasn't another book on the market like it. And I had specialist knowledge from having counseled this client group for years.

When you put together these three elements – service, innovation, and specialist knowledge – what you create is your product. If this is a commercial venture with those three magic elements, people will want to buy your goods or services. If it's a club, people will want to join. If it's a charity, people will want to donate.

There are zillions of businesses that want to sell you food. Many come and go, but the ones that succeed are the ones who have clearly defined the three elements. They have a clear type of client in mind – whether it's a steak-lover, a vegan, someone wanting a snack on the run, or someone wanting haute cuisine. Whatever the client group is, they will lay out their stall to attract that type of eater. They will innovate in terms of their pricing, offers, and types of meals on offer. Their specialist knowledge is in the preparation of the food itself. True, there will be other considerations, such as location, but without those three elements, the restaurant will struggle in even the greatest location.

Technology is an area where the top companies demonstrate their knowledge of the three elements on a grand scale. The founders of these companies changed their lives by changing ours. When I was young, my only experience of using PCs was where you had to start it up in the old DOS operating system. If you are too young to know what I'm talking about, trust me – it was pre-historic.

Then one day I was in a computer store, and the guy who ran it called me over. "See what you think of this," he said. I looked. It was amazing. I had to have it. "I think this is going to be popular," he said.

That was an understatement. I was looking at a Windows operating system for the first time. No wonder Microsoft became the biggest company on the planet. They knew who they wanted to serve: all those frustrated DOS users, millions of them. They innovated in a big way. They had specialist knowledge from having made huge R&D investment.

Some might question why I don't mention marketing as one of the three elements. Surely, marketing is critical? Well, yes and no. Marketing isn't part of the product. The product has to come first. 80% of your effort needs to go into the product. Without a great product, you can market all you like, but you will get found out.

If you have successfully marketed a restaurant, drawing in the crowds, but the food isn't up to scratch, people will leave bad reviews on Trip Advisor and other platforms, and the crowds will start going elsewhere. If you have a restaurant with great food but your marketing isn't so good, you might still thrive, as word of mouth and positive reviews do the work for you.

Yet, it seems so many people spend 80% of their time on marketing. It's so easy to fall into this trap. If you think you need to be on every social media platform, blogging until your keyboard melts, where's your time for being creative, improving your product, and listening to your customers? Who are you serving? Are you focusing on income or service? If you aren't focusing on serving, you are less likely to get income.

You will also need to have good systems backing you up. The money needs to be collected, the bills paid, the computers serviced, and so on. It is tragic if a great product doesn't make it because the admin is a disaster. If this is not your strong point, outsource it, so you can focus on your product.

Realizing that you can create an enterprise from your imagination is life-changing. It was for me. It has allowed me to have more than one career, which has enhanced my life. It has allowed me to react to opportunities. Here's an example:

When I first began playing golf, I was crazy for it. I couldn't get enough. I loved the look of an ocean-side course, the smell of the cut grass, cleaning up my clubs, browsing in golf stores – it had me in its spell. So, when I saw an opportunity to live in one of the world's major golf centers, the Algarve, I went for it. I played every course. I was an expert on the area.

I became fascinated by the phenomenon of golf tourism. Although my local courses were in Portugal, hardly any of the golfers were Portuguese. The majority were from northern Europe, the USA or Canada and were on golf breaks. I started posting information on a website for these visitors: an insider's view of playing in the area. People started asking for help in booking their golf breaks.

I had an idea that I could serve these golfers. My innovation was that I was telling people the unvarnished truth about playing there rather than a lot of sales gloss, and my specialist knowledge came from being a local. I didn't wait until I was ready. I just got on with it. It was just as well I didn't wait because if I had procrastinated and told myself I needed to do more research, I would have discovered just how good the competition was and might have never gone ahead. Sometimes a little ignorance can be a strength.

I was a blur of activity. I got on the phone to the golf courses and started to sign contracts to re-sell tee times. Some golf courses were reluctant, saying they had enough agents, which was probably true, but I was persistent. I did the same thing with hotels, as my golfers would need somewhere to sleep. I signed up with car hire companies and airport transfer companies. I set up a Portuguese company and got an accountancy firm to look after all the legal stuff.

Within days, the first bookings started coming in. Within a couple of weeks, the first customers arrived at the airport. It was hard work, but it was amazing, it was fun. I was playing some of the best golf courses in Europe with my customers. I had momentum and I was living the dream.

I received requests from golfers wanting to play in other areas. So, I expanded the operation, and soon

I had customers arriving across Portugal and neighboring Spain. I had reps meeting them at the airports and transfer companies moving them from one course to another. I had clients from all over Europe and North America. I even taught myself basic German so I could respond to emails in that language. What had started as an idea in my head had become an operation with thousands of golfers arriving annually.

I would, however, like to put in a caveat. You will no doubt have seen the motivational slogan, "Do what you love, and you will never work again". We are advised to monetize our passion. It seems to make sense. You do something you enjoy, and the money will follow.

It would seem that I had done exactly that. Surely there can't be a downside?

Well, maybe.

I loved golf because it had been my release from the day-to-day. It was magical to me. When it became my job, I started to lose that. Imagine a boy who loves watching magic tricks. He grows up and learns to be a magician. He now knows how it works, and he loses the sense of magic – it becomes a job. In the end for me, turning up at a golf course became just like turning up at the office. I stopped playing golf because I had lost the magic. It was 10 years before I picked up my clubs and played again.

So, if you are looking to turn something you love into your work, it's worth considering that you might succeed in a business sense but lose what you love at the same time. And besides, just because you have a passion for something, it doesn't necessarily follow that you will be able to turn it into a successful enterprise. You could be passionate about tennis and want to become a coach. But that doesn't mean you're good, and if you play like a person with two left arms, you will never make it as a tennis coach, no matter how passionate you are.

I suggest that instead of following what it says in motivational memes, instead of thinking about yourself and what you want, I recommend that you think of the kind of people you have a passion to serve. Don't think about yourself, go and serve them.

In my golf business, I succeeded in creating a business with nothing more than my imagination. But I had reached the end of my Path. I realized that I needed a new Path, a new challenge, and new people to serve.

I saw that serving golfers was no longer my passion. Golf and golfers could get along absolutely fine without me. I was just there for the money, and as discussed before in this book, being there just for the money rarely works in the long term. So I left my business.

I find that every few years, the time comes to hit the reset button, and I had reached that point. I needed someone new to serve, and I found those people. I brought my counseling skills and qualifications up-to-date and went to work in part of the health service in the UK. I wrote earlier about being open-minded about outcomes, and when I started on the Path of counseling, I had no idea that the Path would take me to writing this book for you. I just took my Daily Action (turning up for work with a sense of curiosity and enthusiasm) and this is where the Path has taken me.

Life is amazing.

Next, let's remove a major obstacle from your Path to success and happiness.

Taking Off the Filter

Imagine that you had a headset like one of those virtual reality headsets. But this headset is a little different. How it works is that it filters out anything that you don't want to see, and it covers your ears so that it also filters out what you don't want to hear

It doesn't exactly show you virtual reality. Rather, it shows you the version of reality that you would like to be true. It shows you how you think the world should be. (That word "should" is causing trouble yet again.)

It feels good, though. There you are in your little world where everyone and everything agrees with you. It takes away cognitive dissonance: that uncomfortable state of mind when the truth is impinging on what we would prefer to believe. Your mind is at peace. But this headset is a danger to your happiness.

Let's say you have a new love in your life. You think that she (we'll assume it's a woman) is wonderful. You're in love. You want to think that your feelings are being reciprocated. But you can't help noticing that she seems to get a lot of messages. She won't say who they're from, and some nights she disappears and won't answer your call. Your head hurts because reality is suggesting that something is wrong. But you don't want it to be that way. So you put on your headset, and you see and hear only what you want to be true. Isn't that better? No more of that horrible cognitive dissonance. You can relax – until she dumps you, and your headset gets ripped off.

These headsets don't really exist, of course. But they don't need to. Your mind creates them for you without you realizing it. In Cognitive Behavioural Therapy, we call them mental filters. They let in what you want to see, not what is necessarily true, and filter out the rest. They are a menace to your happiness.

Nevertheless, they are alluring because they seem to make sense to the individual. A mental filter offers a comforting point of reference in our ever-changing world because it gives you a fixed viewpoint, and it feels like you have something solid in your life. It's easier to have a fixed view than have to consider a bunch of variables.

Our modern world encourages mental filters. It's so easy to find chat rooms and social media groups for people who have the same mental filter as you do. It could be people with the same political beliefs, religious beliefs, or maybe just people who like the same football team as you. What happens is that you keep reinforcing each other's filters. You come to believe that you must be right and that anyone who disagrees is wrong, so the filter conveniently keeps out other views.

The trouble is that beliefs based on mental filters are spurious and do not serve us. They cause a huge amount of trouble. Mental filters stand between you and total honesty, and if you are not being totally honest with yourself, your success and happiness are at risk. It's like living in a shack in an earthquake zone and assuming nothing could go wrong.

I had a client who opened a little boutique fashion store specializing in one particular label that she adored. She believed that because she felt that way, so would other people, and so the store would be a success. This belief had become a mental filter, and her mind had filtered out evidence that shoppers in the area of her store tended to be price-sensitive, while her label was expensive.

What happened was that shoppers would come in and make positive comments, and her filter would let these comments through as they reinforced her beliefs about the label. But when the same people left the store without spending any money, her filter rejected that piece of vital information as it didn't sit well with her. If the filter had not been in place, she would have seen what was happening and been able to adapt to the client group. But inevitably, the business failed.

Despite the failure, her filter stayed in place, and rather than think of a new, more suitable enterprise, she just became bitter about the shoppers in her area. She called them fools. In fact, they were simply behaving perfectly normally for price-sensitive shoppers. They would look at the clothes in the boutique and make flattering comments because the garments were lovely. But then they would take a look at the price and go and buy at the bargain store around the corner.

By preventing her from seeing the truth about the incompatibility of her products with the local clientele, the filter had undermined both the success and happiness of the boutique owner.

Another client was a great computer salesperson, frequently being the top seller at his dealership. He was bright, articulate, and was seen as good management material. This was the route he wanted his career to go down. But he had a very common problem: he had a fear of public speaking, which meant he got distressed about doing sales presentations within his company, an essential for a manager. His problem wasn't in doing the presentations themselves. He was slick and professional. But he dreaded feedback. He had a deep fear that one day he would say something ridiculous in front of his management and peers that would make him look like an idiot and wreck his career. He was scared of humiliation.

His filter worked in two ways. Firstly, for days before a presentation, it would let through all the fears about things that could go wrong, while filtering out thoughts of everything that could go right. Secondly, if he got a slight criticism of a presentation, his filter would let that through and magnify it, but if he got praise heaped on him, his filter would shut that out as being irrelevant.

Do you have a filter at work in your life, blocking your way to success and happiness?

The difficulty with filters is seeing that they exist in the first place, as people can believe in them passionately. To see this in action, you only have to watch a political debate on television to see mental filters being used full-on. Participants will totally ignore arguments that would undermine their beliefs, as unwanted truths just bounce off the filter.

However, if you have a belief that you suspect might be holding you back, try to prove it. This is what worked with the computer salesperson. I asked him to prove that his fear had a basis in reality. I asked him to pretend he had to present evidence in a court of law to prove his fear had a basis in fact. He could not, and that came as a great relief to him. His fear evaporated. Instead, he worked on achievement stacking, which is much more constructive.

If you can't prove it, that's probably because it's a filter at work. Once you can see through a filter, they lose their power completely. It's like taking off a headset.

Now, let's look at a massive, self-defeating behavior that could be limiting your access to success and happiness.

This Time will be Different

I believe in cause and effect. I believe in actions leading to outcomes. That's science. I also believe that lack of action will have an outcome also, and usually an undesirable one. That's why this book is about embracing change.

Change works if you have a Path with a realistic plan, and you take action in the form of a Daily Action. That keeps you persistently on the Path, and, as they say, persistence pays. And it does pay as long as the plan is realistic. But what if it isn't? What if you are persistently pursuing a misguided goal? How do you know?

In my job as a counselor, I have worked a lot in addiction services, and something that I was up against all the time was the cycle of recovery followed by relapse followed by recovery, and so on ad infinitum. It was tragic to watch. My job was about trying to help people break that cycle once and for all. But it wasn't easy.

Time and time again, you would see people go through the pain of coming off a drug, only to repeat the behaviors that had caused them to relapse previously, such as hanging out with their old friends and going to their old haunts, which would invariably lead to another relapse.

It seems obvious that if you know that doing X always causes Y to happen, and you don't want Y to happen, then you should stop doing X, shouldn't you? It makes total sense. We can all intellectually grasp that.

But we are humans, not machines, and we don't always do what we know intellectually to be true. Frequently, we will work out the best course of action using our brains, but then act based on our emotions and go and do something different. We go and do X all over again.

This is because we want to believe that this time it will be different. We kid ourselves that this time when we do X that Z will happen instead. But it doesn't. As usual, Y happens, and we're back to where we started.

It's not just people in addiction that have this tendency, it's all of us. Because of the power of familiarity, we are attracted to doing what we have done before. It makes doing X seem somehow comforting even though we know deep down that it's a bad idea to do it and that it will hurt us. Then we end up with Y all over again and start beating ourselves up for doing X once more.

What's going on here is that voice in our head is at work again. That voice that doesn't want us to make changes, because it's scared of change. It's telling us that it's okay to do X again because this time it will be different. Even though we know that it isn't true, we end up believing the voice because we want to believe it – it's telling us what we want to hear. It's telling us that we can get a desirable outcome without going through the scariness of change. It's telling us a lie because it doesn't want us to change, as it knows that change has hurt us in the past. But that was when we let change happen to us rather than instigating change, so the voice is misguided.

There is a way out of this cycle. It's a method I have used with a lot of success with clients. It's also a method I use with myself all the time because, even with my training, I am still a human being and make frequent thinking errors. You can't stop it entirely, but you can minimize it. In that way, you experience more success in your life, and we all want that, do we not?

The method I use is called Solution Focused Thinking, or SFT. This has its origins in a form of therapy that psychologists in Milwaukee pioneered towards the end of the last century called Solution Focused Brief Therapy. A brief therapy is one that is used for quick results. It has become one of the key tools for people in my line of work.

But you don't need to be working with a counselor to use SFT. The basic concept, like others in this book, draws strength from being simple. Solution

Focused Thinking can be summed up in two sentences:

Do more of what works for you.

Stop doing what doesn't work.

It sounds so obvious when you look at it. Of course, if you do more of what works and stop doing what doesn't work, you are bound to be more successful. I have managed to achieve much more in my life since I started applying those two sentences to what I'm working on. It's powerful.

In my early days as a therapist, I would reveal this simple concept to clients with a kind of "Ta-Da!" note of triumph. There you go, work these two sentences and your troubles will be over. Yet, I was disappointed with some of my early results.

Solution Focused Thinking is indeed simple, but there is a big difference between simple and easy. Simple concepts still need to be applied. It only works if you actually use it.

If you programmed a computer to apply SFT principals, it would work brilliantly. But we humans have a way of sabotaging ourselves without even realizing we are doing it. That voice in our head starts undermining our best ideas. It's when the mental filter gets in the way. Instead of doing more of what works and stopping what doesn't work, we fall for the old "This time will be different" trick, then repeat our old errors yet again. Let me give you an example.

As you know already, I found it challenging to give up smoking. I become physically dependent on nicotine very easily and once it gets me in its grip, it doesn't let go without a big fight. Every time I stopped smoking, it was painful, and the voice in my head would convince me that it would be okay to smoke just a little bit again, that this time it would be different, and I would be able to smoke on just a casual basis, whenever I chose.

But the voice is a liar. Deep down, I knew it was, yet I wanted to believe it. So, I would pick up something to smoke and become instantly hooked again. And again and again. I was doing X and expecting something other than Y to result. But I always got Y. I was breaking the rules of Solution Focused Thinking because I was repeating what I knew didn't work.

Then, some years ago, I managed to give up. In fact, I gave up for six months. I was convinced I had beaten nicotine. But one day, I was in a bar waiting for a friend who was late, and I noticed individual cigars for sale behind the bar. I thought I could buy one and smoke it while I was waiting. I hadn't smoked in 6 months. What could possibly go wrong?

Well, you're probably ahead of me already. I smoked one cigar, and by the next day, I was back to smoking as much as ever. I had done X and, sure enough, Y followed. The old "This time it will be different" trick had made a fool of me yet again.

It took another 10 years until I finally gave up forever. What a waste of money and how risky for my health. But this time I know it is forever because I finally understand that, when it comes to nicotine and me, X will always produce Y. No exceptions. It will never be different next time.

Solution Focused Thinking invites you to turn all this to your advantage. It invites you to look at your life and see the things that work for you and to do more.

Some people reading this book will be having difficulties right now and might think that nothing is working for them. But if you are having a difficult time, start looking anyway. You will find some things that are going okay. Maybe just little things, but if you start doing more of them, your life will get better.

I'm not talking here about trying to kid yourself into thinking that things are better than they are. I'm not going to suggest that you start putting on a smile when you're dying inside (although it might help). I'm not going to suggest that you recite affirmations that you know you don't mean. This is not kidology. This is looking for the building blocks you can work with to find greater success and happiness. You can turn the whole X and Y argument to your advantage. If Y is an outcome you want, keep doing more of X!

One of my clients was a street musician. Life was tough. He was couch-surfing. He had very little money. His music wasn't going well. Yet, he was a good musician. He had real talent. So, we put together a plan, based on Solution Focused Thinking, to try to turn his fortunes around.

First of all, we looked at where he played. He targeted the train station. It made sense because there was plenty of footfall morning and evening. But, looking at the commuters, you could see why he wasn't doing well with them. People went past him, hands in pockets, looking at their feet, clearly wrapped up in their own world, probably thinking about work and other life issues. They were mostly oblivious to the man with the guitar.

SFT tells us to stop what doesn't work. So, he tried a change. Instead, he targeted the town center at lunchtime, in the area where the restaurants and takeaway food outlets were. His takings went up. I could see why. At lunchtime, people were more relaxed as they had gotten out of work for half an hour. Also, they were out to buy food, so they were already in spending mode, hands on their wallets and purses, and more receptive to getting out a coin for the musician. Things were looking up.

Then we looked at what he played. He usually played his own compositions, which were good, but people didn't know them and didn't connect to them. So, he experimented with playing music from different genres. What he found worked best was old pop and rock classics, the sort of stuff that people knew from childhood, and in particular songs that were cheerful or inspiring. So, if he played the Beatles' "Here Comes the Sun" or Bon Jovi's "It's My Life". The money poured in. So, he played more of that. He did more of what worked.

Finally, he tried putting some information about himself on a board. It was just things like his name, where he came from, and how old he was. He noticed that people who stopped to read his brief bio would leave money. You can see why. Passers-by were now able to connect with him on a human level. He was no longer just another anonymous street musician. So, he made his board bigger and had more personal information. It worked. He got together enough money for a rental deposit for somewhere to live, and his life was taking off. He has simply applied the SFT principals to his situation.

I have realized from working with clients that the main difficulty people face in applying Solution Focused Thinking in their lives is that what works for them is not what they want it to be. A great example of this is the work I have done with problem drinkers. For 90% of them, stopping drinking, at least for a while, is the action they need to do more of in order to break the cycle of recovery followed by relapse. But they almost always want to cut down rather than stop, although it has never worked for them before. They cling to the belief that it will be different this time, and that this time X will result in Z. But that never happens. The drinkers who succeed are the ones who ignore the voice in their head, throw away the filter, and are totally honest with themselves about what works.

Being totally honest with yourself, even when the truth is not what you think you want, is hugely empowering. What we think we want and what we truly need are often very different. So, how do we get totally honest with ourselves, when our minds are playing tricks on us to persuade us to take a different path?

Here is an experiment you can run with yourself right now that will help you to be totally honest with yourself and see clearly where you need to put your efforts in life.

For the rest of today (or from tomorrow morning, if you are reading this late in the day) try to be aware of every time an opinion comes into your mind. It doesn't matter what it's an opinion on. You might be surprised by just how many opinions you have. Then look at your opinion and ask yourself: "Is this really true? Could I prove this under oath? Or is this just an illusion or wishful thinking?"

This is an exercise that will teach you a lot about how your mind works. If you do this just for one day, you will strengthen your decision-making skills forever and will make it easier for you to get more success and happiness into your life.

I imagine that most people reading this won't try it. It's human nature. Readers will think, "I must try that sometime," but sometime never comes. That's your prerogative. You paid for this book (thank you!) and it's up to you to use it as you see fit. But for those of you who try this experiment, you will change your life today.

Around and Around

I love running therapeutic workshops. Getting together with a group of clients and bouncing around the issues of the day is highly stimulating. I always have a plan for a workshop, of course, but that plan includes provision for spontaneity and reaction to new issues that people bring along.

One concept that emerged from a workshop is what we called the Spinning Wheels of Anxiety and Depression. I have used this concept many times since, and it always resonates with people. That's not surprising, as all human beings experience anxiety to some extent, and we experience depression sometimes. (By depression, I'm talking about what people colloquially mean when they say they are depressed: low mood, feelings of negativity, and lack of self-worth. I am not talking about serious clinical depression, which requires psychiatric support and medication, and is beyond the scope of this book.)

In that original workshop, people in the group all said that they suffered from anxiety or depression regularly. It disturbed their sleep. It made them feel worried and agitated at random times for no apparent reason. Often, they would feel this way in the morning and could not shake the feelings off for hours. They would end up losing all their productive time that day. If you ever feel like that, then this chapter is for you.

Our minds are great problem-solving machines. To see this is true, you only have to look around the room you are in. Everything from the paint on the walls to the apps on your phone are amazing examples of how humans have solved mega-zillions of problems to create the world we live in. It is who we are as a species. We love to solve problems and create new things. We even do problem-solving puzzles for recreation.

If you ask your mind to solve a question, it will go off and do it for you. It might not be able to give you an instant response, but it will keep trying until it comes up with an answer.

It must have happened to you at some time that you were trying to remember the name of a person from the past, or the name of an old TV show, or the title of a song. Even if you consciously give up (and don't cheat by using Google) your unconscious mind will keep on the case. Then at a later time, when you had consciously forgotten about the question, the answer will suddenly pop up into your mind. Your subconscious has done its job.

Similarly, when you face a problem you cannot solve consciously, your subconscious will keep working on it for you. Then all of a sudden, often when you weren't even thinking about it, a new insight or answer will come bounding into your conscious mind.

This is all wonderful and amazing, but there is one snag: your mind has its limits, and if it tries to go beyond its limits, it will start thoughts spinning around in your head. Your mind doesn't always recognize the difference between what is solvable and what is impossible. It will go around and around in circles, trying to answer questions that cannot be solved.

Take the big eternal questions about existence – the "Why am I here?" type questions. Your mind has no more chance of working out these big questions than your cat has of understanding how your car works. Yet, if you ask your mind to try, it will have a go anyway. But you will give yourself mental torment. We humans have got around these limitations by creating religions and philosophies to help us cope.

So, what has all this to do with my workshop on anxiety and depression? Simply this: if you set your mind an insoluble problem, it will go ahead and try to solve it anyway, leading to mental misery.

If a bad event has happened in your past that cannot be changed, you might wish it had never happened. However, when you wish for that, your mind takes up the challenge of trying to put it right for you. It will never succeed because it cannot go into the past and change what has happened. But it will try. The result will be you constantly mulling over past events, generating feelings of anger, resentment, despair, loss, and maybe even self-loathing. It's a horrible place to be, especially at night when you want to sleep but cannot because the same thoughts keep spinning around your head in an endless spiral of torment.

At the workshop, I drew a big circle on a flip-chart. The circle was there to represent the mind spinning endlessly, trying to resolve a problem. I asked the group how they would label that circle. They agreed it should be labeled "Past Pain", and I wrote that in the middle of the circle.

I then wrote the words "If only" and "What if". This comes up when you ask yourself (and therefore your subconscious) questions like: "What if that had never happened?" or "If only I had done something different." And your subconscious gets on with trying to solve something beyond its capabilities, resulting in you suffering more anguish and lost sleep. Underneath the circle, I wrote "Depression", as depression comes from trying to resolve past pain.

Then I drew a second circle, and put the question, "How about if we ask "If only" or "What if" for things that haven't happened, such as "If only that wouldn't happen" or "What if the worst does happen? How should that be labeled.

The group decided that should be labeled "Future pain". They were exactly right, so I wrote that in the middle of the second circle.

This is where your mind projects ahead to events that haven't occurred and may never occur. Your mind ruminates on the pain you might experience. Sometimes this is entirely logical. For example, if you have a dental appointment, you know that there will be some discomfort, no matter how good your dentist might be. But if your mind is ruminating on, let's say, the emotional and financial pain you might experience if you lose your job, when your job is quite safe, then it's a pointless waste of your time.

I understand this experience of ruminating on future events that might not even happen, as my mind loves to do this – especially in the middle of the night. It's a nuisance. But more than that, this rumination can produce real fear. Take for example someone who is anxious about flying. For most of us, flying is routine. I enjoy it. But someone who has a flying phobia will start to experience real fear if they have to fly somewhere. Their mind will be projecting ahead all sorts of disasters and even death. They will not be sleeping well.

This ruminating on future pain is where anxiety comes from. So, we have our two spinning circles: one is ruminating on the past and is depression; the other is ruminating on the future and is anxiety.

So, having understood where depression and anxiety come from, what can we do about it?

Well, if the past and the future cause pain or mental discomfort, how about the present?

As you are reading a book on personal change, you probably have issues in your life, maybe serious ones. But how are you right now, this very moment? Most people make themselves comfortable when reading, so it's quite likely that you are in a good place, such as on your sofa, in bed, relaxing during a work-break, or maybe you are even reading this next to the pool on vacation. If you are listening to the audiobook version, you could be walking your dog, working out in the gym, or preparing a meal.

My point is that right at this exact moment, you are probably okay while reading this book. Your life will have had past pain, and your future will bring new challenges. But right now, in the present, you might well be fine – at least for now.

We hear a lot about living in the moment, and there's a great deal of sense in this. After all, if your focus is on the present moment, your mind cannot be causing you depression by mulling over past events, and it cannot be causing you anxiety by ruminating on the future. It's impossible if you are focused on the present, since your conscious mind cannot focus on two things simultaneously.

This makes being in the here-and-now very desirable because while we are focused on the present, we aren't experiencing past pain or future fear. But how do we achieve this focus on the present when our mind is trying to drag us in other directions?

The answer is right here in this book. We have already discussed at length having a Path and a Daily Action. If you have a Path, you know that as long as you take your Daily Action, you will reach the end of your Path. No other outcome is possible. This greatly reduces projecting ahead. If the end of your Path is ahead and you cannot get lost, what's there to worry about? And by focusing on your Daily Action, your mind will stop dwelling on past pain or future fear. You cannot focus on your Daily Action and think about the past or the future at the same moment – it's impossible.

Another way to keep your mind in the present is to focus on what is going well in your life just now. Most of the clients I have worked with have been in the midst of a crisis. People don't come to me for help when their lives are cruising along just fine. Usually, something bad has happened or is happening.

126

When I put to a client the question, "So, what's going right for you just now?" I am often met with astonishment, and people will say things like, "Nothing! My life's a mess." But when we look carefully, even in the midst of crisis, there is always something going right. It might be small things. But there are always good things.

I'm not talking about having a positive attitude or practicing gratitude (although those things have a lot going for them). What I mean is looking closely for the good stuff that's working to give yourself some building blocks to start constructing some peace of mind.

Try writing a list of things that are okay in your life right now. Make it a long list. Go for a hundred things. What do you have to wear that you like? What have you to eat that you like? Who has been kind to you lately? Is your favorite show on TV later? If you are feeling down, try it now. It will help you shift your perspective and keep you in the present.

Obsessed with Addiction

You have already discovered that I have done a lot of work in the field of addiction. Indeed you might even have read books I have written on the subject. I would include obsessions in with this. The difference is just the choice of words. Addiction carries with it some negative associations. Obsession just doesn't sound quite as bad.

But this is not a book about addiction, you might think, so why am I writing about it here?

The answer is that this is a book about success and happiness, and addictions and obsessive behaviors are major blocks to your personal development. If an obsession or addiction gets out of hand, it can be like a wrecking ball, smashing up your life.

If you say the word addict to most people, the first thing that comes to their mind is a drug-user. But this is misleading. We are all addicts to some extent. It's part of being human.

It's amazing just how many things we human beings can get addicted to. Here are some that spring to mind:

- Gambling
- Sex
- Drinking

- Sugar
- Shopping
- Approval
- Video games
- Smartphones
- Cigarettes
- People
- Social media
- Prescription drugs
- Exercising
- Watching television
- Bodybuilding
- Shoplifting
- Salt
- Work
- Speed
- Coffee
- Arson
- Tattoos
- Praise
- Dieting
- Binge eating
- Taking risks
- Plastic surgery
- Hoarding

That's a long list, and you could add to it almost endlessly because there will be someone, somewhere addicted to just about anything you can think of.

So, what exactly is an addict or an addiction? After all, some of the things on the list above seem perfectly fine. What could possibly be wrong with watching television or exercising, for instance?

It's a question of degree. If you have an activity or interest in your life that you take to an extent where it's harming you, then you have reached the point where your happiness is being eroded.

Take, for example, collecting. We humans like to collect things. Most people have a little collection of something. Children in particular love to collect. If you are a parent, you will know what I mean. Your child comes home in a state of uncontrollable excitement about some new thing that the kids at school are collecting and won't be able to rest until he or she has some, too. They badger you for money and to take them to the store or go online to get some of whatever it might be. Then a few weeks later, another collecting craze will sweep the school. Do you remember Pokémon cards, Minecraft and Warhammer? Kids went crazy for those.

When I was a boy, I was the same. Like most boys I knew, I went through phases of collecting football cards and stamps. At one point, I got interested in Roman coins. I spent my pocket money on the more common coins that I could afford. I got involved. I learned a lot about Roman history. Then I lost interest. I can't remember what distracted me

– probably girls or playing guitar. I guess I was a pretty ordinary boy.

There was nothing wrong with my collecting Roman coins. It was harmless, and I learned some history. But what if it had got out of hand? What if I had got so obsessed that my schoolwork had suffered? What if I had started stealing money from my parents so I could buy more coins? What if I had started lying to cover up the extent of my obsession? What if it had let me into hoarding?

When I was working in counseling, I was approached about working with hoarders. I must admit that my first reaction was negative. I didn't see hoarding as being something that needed professional help. But Sonia changed my mind about that.

If you saw Sonia in the street, you might think she was a bag lady, but she had a large house where she lived alone. Her concerned family had referred her. They said her hoarding had taken over her life and she was neglecting herself. Our first approaches to Sonia were rebuffed. She didn't want anyone around her house. She was covering up. After several counseling sessions with a patient worker, however, she relented and agreed to let workers in.

The house was full of just about anything you can imagine. And I do mean full. There was nowhere to sit and hardly anywhere to stand. There were piles of magazines that were taller than Sonia herself. And it didn't stop at the house. Sonia had run out of space in the house, so she had started burying things in the garden. It was then that she had begun questioning what she was doing. She had seen through her filter, which was why she had decided to accept help.

Some people would just write Sonia off as being a crazy old lady, but that would be wrong. She was addicted to collecting. She would collect anything. Far from being crazy, she was mentally very sharp in certain ways. She had an amazing memory. Someone coming into her house would just see a huge mess – but not Sonia. She knew everything she had and where everything was. It was incredible. Her brain was like a huge library where she stored the locations of all her items.

Sonia is, admittedly, an extreme example, but I use her story to make a point. The difference between my collecting Roman coins and Sonia being a self-neglecting obsessive is just a question of degree.

My definition of an addiction is thus:

The pursuit of one particular source of pleasure to the detriment of other vital aspects of life.

By vital aspects of life, I mean things like having healthy relationships, maintaining personal standards, health, career, and finances. If these things start to suffer because someone is pursuing an obsession with drinking, gambling, eating, traveling, buying things they can't afford, or whatever it might be, then you have found an addict, and the pleasure they are pursuing is their addiction.

Does this describe someone in your life? Indeed, does it describe you?

It certainly describes me. I've already written about my nicotine addiction. But there have been others, some worse than others. At one time, my obsession with golf would come close to meeting my definition of an addiction. At another time, I was just as obsessed with fly fishing. That might sound harmless enough, but at one point I was spending all my money and neglecting my career and family just so I could catch fish. It sounds crazy now, but I was obsessed.

So coming back to my earlier list, can watching television, for instance, really be classed as an addiction? Again, it's a question of degree. If you watch for an hour in the evening to unwind, no it isn't an addiction. But if you spend half your life watching television to the detriment of your relationships and profession, if your health is suffering because you get no exercise and spend most of your time on the couch in front of the television munching pizza, then it meets my definition of an addiction.

So, how come we can get obsessed or addicted to such a wide variety of things? And how come some people get addicted to substances they put in their bodies – anything from caffeine to cocaine – whereas other people get addicted to an action, such as running?

Science isn't conclusive on addictions – it is a challenging thing to analyze. But one theory that has widespread acceptance in science, and makes sense to me, is that it it involves neurotransmitters. These are chemical messengers in the brain. There are several of these, but when it comes to obsessional or addictive behavior, it seems the important one is dopamine.

When released in your brain, dopamine makes you feel good, which is why it can create addictions. Quite why different things cause dopamine release in different people is unclear. It just seems to be human diversity. But it explains why some people can get addicted to certain behaviors, such as gambling, whereas others get addicted to substances, such as sugar. The common factor is that they produce a burst of dopamine in some people, and the person feels good. So they want to get it again and end up with a compulsive behavior.

It even explains why people can get obsessed with other people. If you get a dopamine rush when you see a person, you might get obsessed with them.

There is a lot of similarity between addiction and love, which is where co-dependency comes from.

The downside with dopamine is that it is short term. It might seem great because it makes you feel good, but it doesn't produce long-term happiness (serotonin does that, which we'll discuss later). An extreme example is crack cocaine, which sends dopamine levels up to 70 times normal, but only for a few minutes, which is why people can spend a fortune on crack because they want to get that feeling back again and again. But you don't have to take hard drugs to get a dopamine rush. Some people might get that rush from eating ice cream – but just not to the same extent as crack, or Ben and Jerry's would be the biggest company on the planet.

If you have an obsession or addiction holding you back from achieving success or happiness in your life, what can you do about it?

You can start by using the "Why is that?" technique we learned early in this book. Put your obsession to the test. Taking the example of the television addict, ask "Why is that?" The answer might be that the person is bored. But then ask, "Why is that?" again, and keep digging down to the real reason and find the hidden desire.

Once you have done that, you can start constructing your Path to your true desire. The key to overcoming an obsession or addiction is usually in finding something you want more, and something good for you that will produce that success and happiness. Giving up an obsession or addiction is like giving up someone you love but you know is bad for you, so you need something fabulous instead. Or you will go back to you're your old love and all the problems that brings.

If you have an addiction problem and don't know what that something you want more could be, you might like to revisit the chapter It All Starts with Desire.

But first, I want you to meet Terry.

A Taste to Die For

I had a new client called Terry. His wife referred him to me as she was worried about his health and, in particular, his weight. This was an unusual referral for me, as I am not a doctor or nutritionist, I am a counselor. But she felt I was the right person for him to see, since she believed his problem was more in his head than his stomach.

I invited Terry to attend one of my cognitive therapy-based groups, but he was horrified at this. He said he would like to come and see me when there was no one around – an unusual request. So, I met Terry at the end of the day when most people had already left the building.

Terry was a pleasant and well-mannered 59-year-old. But he was clearly overweight. He wore capacious track-suit bottoms as he would have difficulty with normal trousers, and he wore oversize Croc sandals because his feet were swollen.

He told me that he had been able to retire at 50. Since then, he had piled on the weight. He said he had a holiday home on the coast that he often visited with his wife. I knew where he was referring to. It was a beautiful area where I often used to go walking myself. But he didn't like to go out during the day because he was embarrassed about his weight. This was why he had asked to see me when the building was quiet. It caused problems for his wife, who often had to go out alone because he didn't want to be seen.

I had met his wife. She was trim and liked walking. She dearly wished her husband would join her on walks out in the countryside. But his social embarrassment, coupled with his lack of mobility due to his size, meant that this wasn't possible, which just added to Terry's embarrassment about himself.

Terry talked about his fears for the future. He was worried that because of his weight, he wouldn't live much longer. He was worried his wife would leave him as he didn't participate fully in their life together. He had a lot of motivation to take action. Yet he did not.

When he described his typical day's eating, it became clear why. He said he loved meat with rich sauces and all the trimmings. He loved eating out, the shiny cutlery, gleaming glasses, and chatting with the waiter. He loved to wash it all down with copious amounts of alcohol. He ate eye-watering amounts.

But it wasn't so much what he said as the way he said it that caught my attention. Although his eating was the root cause of all his problems and he knew it was killing him, he spoke of it with such passion. When he said he loved his food, he really meant he loved it. His wife wished he spoke about her with so much passion.

When we talked about taking action about his eating, Terry became very defensive. This might seem odd, as this was exactly what he said he wanted to do. But when we spoke about reduction, there was a look of panic on his face. I knew that look from my work in addiction services. It was the same look of panic you see if you suggest coming off a methadone prescription to an opiate user, or if you suggest giving up the booze to an alcoholic.

Terry didn't just love his food – he was addicted to it.

Terry's passion for food fitted my definition of an addiction: The pursuit of one particular source of pleasure to the detriment of other vital aspects of life. Although Terry intellectually understood the danger his eating was putting him in, his addiction was overriding his common sense. He just couldn't stop himself. He was dying because of the tastes he loved so much.

When a chef designs a dish for his customers, he chooses a combination of ingredients that will please them. He wants their business. What he is really doing is selecting a combination of tastes that will light up the pleasure centres in the brain and release the neurotransmitters that give us a feeling of pleasure.

Within food manufacturing companies, creating the tastes that will release those neurotransmitters gets even more technical. It's not only chefs that are involved, but food scientists are also. The complex combinations of salts, fats, sugars and other additives are tested and thoroughly market-researched. When you are making product-release decisions in big food companies or restaurant chains, billions of dollars are at stake.

Companies try to get just the right amount of salt, fat and sugar in products to create something called the Bliss Point. This is where the taste lights up your pleasure senses, but without totally satisfying the desire for salt, fats and sugar, so you crave more, and a desire to overeat is created. Small wonder that so many of us in the West struggle with our weight when food manufacturers are deliberately trying to turn us into addicts. The food industry has a word for making food addictive: optimizing.

I can relate to the addictive nature of processed food. Put a packet of some kind of potato chips in my hand and I have to finish the packet. The safest thing for my waistline is not to open the packet in the first place.

Terry's conversation went between extremes: sometimes lamenting what his eating was doing to himself, then, often in the next breath, defending his eating. This seems illogical. It was like Terry was arguing with himself. In fact, he was arguing with his addiction, and much of the time I felt like a bystander, cheering on Terry when he started to win the argument.

You always knew when the addiction was winning because Terry would start worrying about protein. "Where will I get my protein from if I stop eating sausage?" he would exclaim. I explained that Terry's main problem with protein is that he ate far too much of it, he ate enough protein to keep an army platoon going on maneuvers. But he couldn't accept that.

So, Terry would use this to defend his eating, even though he knew the damage it was doing to him. This conflict of logic, cognitive dissonance, is common in people with addictions, and it drives people crazy until they can see through the filter. In Terry's case, the filter was filtering out the truth of what his eating was doing and letting in all the wishful-thinking arguments for carrying on as he was.

Terry was caught in a classic addiction trap. He ate because it made him happy in the short term – the dopamine released by the tastes did that – but it was conversely destroying his long-term happiness because he hated looking in the mirror and seeing what it was doing to him.

A direct link exists between good health and happiness. To an extent, you have to play with the cards that genetics has dealt you. Also, you cannot go back in time and undo any damage you might have done to yourself. Your health might have been compromised by sheer bad luck if you have caught an infectious disease or been the victim of an accident. But you can accept where you are now and make a start to change your life today.

Terry's solution was to commit to a long-term Path of change and take the Daily Action of cutting out all the high-calorie fatty foods that gave him the short-term dopamine buzz. As his overall happiness increased, he found that it became more important than the tastes that were killing him.

Let's look at how Terry or anyone can achieve that.

Weighing Up Success

In doing my research for this book, I found that diet and weight maintenance were related issues people particularly wanted to address. I feel this is an important area for this book as a successful change in this area leads to more happiness for three reasons:

What you eat and drink affects the chemical balance in your body and brain. It can take your mood up or down and also cause your mood to change with more or less volatility. In other words, it affects the chemistry that controls your happiness.

If you eat a diet that is good for you, then you will have far less anxiety about suffering from sickness and disease. This peace of mind helps facilitate contentment and happiness.

We all like to approve of what we see in the mirror. I'm not saying you should conform to some stereotypical view of what is attractive. That's really setting yourself up to fail. But if you are comfortable with your appearance, that will add to your feeling of confidence, enhancing success and happiness.

So, in this chapter, we'll look at applying the concepts in this book to losing weight or keeping your weight in balance if you are happy as you are.

Fortunately, I have found a single plan that achieves both aims. I have confidence in what you are about to read, as it's not just theory – I have proved it to myself.

Passions often run high when we talk about food, as you will see if you join a few food-related social media groups. People end up trading insults from their entrenched, dogmatic positions on food. It can get political and for some people, even religion comes into food.

But I'm a pragmatist with a background working in healthcare, so I look for what works, not what fits a political agenda. I look for what is backed up by quality scientific research. The following is what I discovered, and I share it with you now as it might change your life for the better.

When I was in my early twenties, I had a naturally active lifestyle. I lived in London and got around the city on the underground train system. That meant I did a lot of walking, either between home and the local station or between other stations and my destinations. I also used to be on my feet most of the time at work. I remember I ate reasonably healthily at home, and I didn't earn that much, so I ate at home rather than buying expensive takeouts.

I can see from photos of me from back then that I didn't have a weight problem – I was a stick.

That changed in my mid-twenties. I moved out of London, got a car and started driving everywhere. I got an office-based job and spent much of my day in a chair. I also had the money to buy fast food. Almost without my noticing, the weight started to pile on. Pretty soon, I was going up in trouser sizes. My life got busy with work and a young family. I neglected my health in favor of a convenience food lifestyle, eating in the car on the go instead of just eating at proper mealtimes. I thought that I must do something about my weight, but before I knew it, years had gone by, and the weight stayed on.

Then a few years ago, I tried to get a grip on the problem. I realized that as I was getting older, I needed to take action, or I would be overweight all my life. I looked into various ways of losing weight. There's no shortage of people out there willing to give advice, but as anyone reading this that has been in the same position will know, there is so much conflicting advice. And it can't all be correct.

I was as confused as everyone else. So, I set out to look at the whole business of controlling my weight from scratch, trying to use Solution-Focused Thinking to help me. I started by looking at cutting out sugar. Many people have success in weight management by cutting out sweet things. But I realized that wasn't my problem. Cutting out sugar didn't make much of a difference because I've never had a particularly sweet tooth. But I love savory things. I loved sausages, bacon, chorizo, cheese, and pastry-covered savories, My favorite meat was pork, especially the fattier cuts. It's not surprising weight was a problem. I tried various ways to cut down my calorie intake, but I just got hungry and would blow it.

Then I read up on low-carb style diets. Book shops and blogs were bursting with advice on this subject and still are. I tried Atkins and other similar diets that have followed it, like the low-carb, high-meat Keto and Paleo diets. I liked the idea of a diet that would appeal to my savory tastes. I had a few goes at this type of dieting, and it worked a bit, but then I would just put the weight back on.

One thing that puzzled me was that I would eat enough to feel full, yet I still craved food. Why was that? I couldn't figure it out. Also, I found this kind of diet seemed counterintuitive: I couldn't help feeling that a diet that was high in fat must be bad for me. It seems I was right to be suspicious, as since then I have looked into what major scientific studies have concluded, which is that these low-carb diets are dangerous, with an elevated risk of premature death.

For instance, research on data from 24,825 participants in the U.S. National Health and Examination Survey showed that people with the lowest intake of carbs had a 50% higher risk of death from a heart attack or stroke than those consuming the most carbs. It sounded like a low-carb diet is something I should be avoiding!

However, if I was to avoid the low-carb route, this left me without a plan. In terms of working a Path, I could not get going. Remember the "P" in Path stands for planning, but I could not find the right plan. I had tried working things out for myself and simply counting calories, but I constantly came up against the problem of bingeing when I got hungry. Bingeing is a flaw I have that I have to work around. I rarely eat chocolate, for instance, but give me a box of chocolates, and I will want to eat the lot in one sitting. I am also the kind of person who finds it hard to leave food on the plate, even when I know I'm full. So, my attempts at controlling calories always ended up in a binge.

If controlling calories didn't work and diets like the Keto were downright dangerous, then I couldn't work a Path until I found a plan that was binge-proof. My breakthrough came when I discovered the writings of Dr. John McDougall.

McDougall is an American physician who went to work at a sugar plantation in Hawaii when he first qualified to practice. His patients were immigrants from Asia who had come to work there. They had brought with them their traditional way of eating, based on grains, vegetables and fruit. McDougall realized that the older people, who stuck to their traditional diet, were generally slim, fit and healthy, avoiding common western diseases, including obesity, and living to an active old age.

By contrast, their children and grandchildren had started eating the usual western diet of processed foods, based on refined carbohydrates, meat, and dairy. These younger people were fatter than their elders and suffered from all the common diseases that plague the west, like diabetes, heart disease and various cancers.

McDougall saw that as these people had the same genes, it must be the western diet that was making the younger people fatter and less healthy. So, he set about learning how he could treat patients using diet rather than prescribing drugs.

Inspired by the traditional diet of the fit, older generation he had encountered, he encouraged patients to eat foods that were high in nutrients but low in fat. He was seen as a maverick at the time, but since then science has increasingly supported his views about diet to the extent that it is now mainstream. This has taken time – his first book on the subject was published in 1983. His work is no fad. It has stood the test of time.

The health benefits of the diet-based treatment that McDougall had trail-blazed were impressive, and we'll look more at health in the next chapter.

But what caught my attention was that McDougall's original recommendations had been for general health, not weight loss. Yet his patients found they lost weight as a by-product of adopting McDougall's healthy eating program. Then, by making the change in their eating habits permanent, rather than going on a short-term weight-loss program, they could manage their weight for good.

Up to that point, I had haphazardly gleaned my knowledge of diet, reading an article here and there. The same is probably true of most people. This is how I had picked up on the idea that somehow carbs were bad, and fat and protein were good. But McDougall explained that an adult man like me needs only 20 grams of protein and 3 grams of fat daily. These are not large amounts. Most people already consume far more than this.

By contrast, the same average male needs 700 grams of carbohydrates to meet his energy requirements, according to McDougall.

However, it's vital to understand that not all carbs are equal and healthy. Carbohydrates from whole grains and vegetables are good for your health and help you feel full while being naturally low in calories. And as they take a while to digest, they keep you satisfied for longer.

The so-called refined carbs are a different matter. These are carbohydrates stripped of all their goodness and these are the types of carbs that are found in white bread, pastries, cakes, and fast-food products made with white flour. Refined carbs are poor in nutrient content and are digested quicker, so you feel hungry again sooner.

Wholegrain carbs are better for your mood. As they release slower, you get less insulin-spiking in your bloodstream, which will help you stay feeling calmer and more balanced.

As a counselor, I have found this knowledge useful in helping me to serve my clients better. My training was all about using cognitive therapy, essentially looking at how people think and how this could be adjusted to help them lead better lives. This is great, as it does work.

However, it isn't always someone's thinking skills that are the total problem. In recent times, I have asked questions about the client's diet during the initial assessment because, if the client's mood problems are a consequence of their diet causing wild insulin spikes, then using cognitive therapy is going to be a waste of time.

In short, what you put in your body affects your mental health as well as your physical health. So, someone might feel like they have a mood disorder when what is really happening is that the sugars and additives in what they are eating are messing around with their dopamine levels, causing highs and lows.

So, I got into the idea of wholefoods rather than processed foods. For a lot of people, wholefood has cranky overtones. But it's not like that at all. Again, it's just common sense. A useful definition of wholefood is something that has had nothing bad added and nothing good taken away.

Take, for instance, an apple. If you eat an apple, you are eating the whole of the food. But if you drink apple juice, that is not a wholefood, as something good had been taken away: in throwing away the pulp of the apple, you are also throwing away the important dietary fiber. If you turn your apple into an apple pie, you are probably going to be adding sugar and also refined carbs to the pastry, so it's no longer a wholefood.

Sometimes the difference is less obvious. Peanut butter, for example, by definition has been processed to turn it from a solid nut to a spreadable paste. Many brands of peanut butter contain lots of oils and other additives and are processed food. But if you make your peanut butter from 100% peanuts, which some brands are, then you have not added anything bad or taken away anything good, so it still fits the definition of wholefood.

McDougall cleared up for me the mystery of why I would still want to eat on a low-carb diet, even though my stomach felt full. He explained that if your body was short of carbohydrates, you would get cravings for it, although your stomach might be full. That explained why I could eat my fill of chicken, for example, but still want more to eat. It wasn't that I simply wanted more food: my body was telling me it needed more carbohydrates for my energy needs, and meat doesn't give you that.

I did some more research, reading the writings of other important writers that have come along since McDougall began his work, like Dr. Joel Fuhrman and Dr. Michael Greger. If nutrition interests you, I recommend reading their work.

These writers disagree on a few points, but on the overall thrust of their work, there is great agreement: eat a nutrient-rich, plant-based, wholefood diet and you will get healthier, and if you need to lose weight, that will happen without the need to go on a calorie-restricted diet. As long as you stick to vegetables, legumes and whole grains, cut out oils and processed foods, eat nuts and fruit in small but regular amounts, and greatly limit your intake of animal products, you can eat as much as you like.

Eat as much as you like?

That sounded like the diet for me!

It's easy to see why this works. For example, an average cheeseburger, minus the bun, contains 303 calories per 100 grams. If you imagine how big a single cheeseburger is without the bun and imagine how much space it would take up in your stomach, you can see that it would not fill you up. That's why you need the bun as well. If you add to that a portion of fries and maybe a milkshake to wash it down, before you know it, you're over 1,000 calories.

Compare that to a vegetable – let's say spinach – which contains 27 calories per 100 grams, and you see why you can eat a heck of a lot of plant-based foods and feel full without racking up lots of calories. True, you wouldn't just eat spinach, but you can see that just a few hundred calories of any combination of vegetables is going to fill you. It simply makes sense.

So at last, I had my plan: I was going to commit to a high-nutrient, low-fat diet. My Daily Action was to eat this way every day. I decided in advance that I would allow myself a bit of slack – I wasn't going to beat myself up if I ate a slice of white bread occasionally, for example – but it was important for me to be honest with myself, so any exceptions I made to my new way of eating were few. I also decided to be open about my outcomes. I wasn't going to set myself a target date to get to a certain weight. Instead, I would focus on my Daily Action of eating healthily and let nature do its thing.

I had some decisions to make first, though. Firstly, was I going to eat meat? In McDougall's writing, he suggests eating meat just on special occasions, what he calls feast days. Joel Fuhrman suggests using meat as a garnish rather than the main part of the meal if you just can't get along without the taste of it.

The decision to cut out processed foods that contained meat was easy when I looked at the facts. There is now a big body of scientific research that shows that processed foods made with red meat could be as harmful to your health as smoking. That's frightening. I didn't go through the pain of giving up smoking just to kill myself with sausages. Okay, that meant I would have to give up sausages and bacon, and I did like the taste, just like Terry in the last chapter. But I asked myself, which would I prefer: a life without the taste of processed meat or the worry of a fatal disease?

Easy choice.

I decided the simplest thing to do was to just stay off red meat altogether, and maybe have a little lean poultry occasionally if I got desperate for the taste of something that wasn't vegetable-based.

I also decided to keep a little fish and seafood in my diet, especially the small stuff at the bottom of the food chain, like prawns, sardines and mackerel. These little items are big on important nutrients, notably certain types of omega-3s, and are also less likely to be affected by marine pollutants than fish higher up the food chain.

When you look at leaving things out of your diet, you could feel that you're depriving yourself, which is a major reason why diets fail. We don't like to feel we are missing out. But in changing my diet, I had a lot of eating to do just to consume all the things that were recommended, so I was never hungry and had few cravings for things I had cut out.

The last difficulty I had to plan around was being able to stick to my new eating plan during busy times. It was easy enough at home, but during the day, I was working in a busy outpatient wing of a hospital, and I didn't have time to prepare food at work. I had been in the habit of going out to grab something for lunch from local stores in the town.

I quickly saw that it was not going to be easy to find ready-to-eat food that fitted my new eating plan. Shelf after shelf was stacked with processed food snacks, most containing meat. Even the ones that didn't contain meat weren't great choices – a processed food snack that doesn't contain animal products might be better than one that does, but it's still processed food, probably with added salt, oil, so not ideal. I even found I had to be wary of pre-prepared salads, as they usually came with dressings that pushed the calorie count up dramatically.

So, as part of my plan, my Daily Action included preparing food at home to take to work. I discovered I enjoyed foods that I would previously never have dreamed of eating. My default snack to take to work was spinach, rocket, spicy salsa and low-fat hummus rolled up together in a whole-wheat wrap, burrito-style. A far cry from the pastry-covered, meaty snacks I used to live on.

Finally, to keep my motivation going, I kept reading books by the previously-mentioned authors and watched videos by them.

I had done my research and planning. Next, I just needed to keep doing the Daily Actions to take me down my Path.

So, did it work?

Yes, it did. I lost thirty pounds. It took a few months, but as I was never hungry, I was never at serious risk of blowing it and bingeing, which is what had always happened when I had tried to lose weight in the past. What's more, I've been happy to make permanent changes to my way of eating. It's easy because over time your tastes change anyway, and also the health benefits of this way of eating are massively motivating.

On the subject of which, let's look at staying healthy.

Healthy Ever After

Feeling healthy – or at least as healthy as we can feel, given our genes, our age, or any diseases we might succumb to through bad luck – has to be top of the list of ways to stay happy. It also massively increases your being successful because the better you feel, the better you will perform at whatever you want to be good at. And it doesn't have to be difficult. Some health hacks are ridiculously easy to implement. Let's look at an example.

If I told you I had a substance that if you took enough of it daily would greatly reduce your chances of having a heart attack, stroke, or getting type-2 diabetes, would you take it? You might be a bit skeptical. You might be concerned that it would be hugely expensive or have side effects. If a drug company could come up with a pill that would do that, they would charge big money for it, and it would make them billions. It would become one of the most successful drugs of all time.

But how about if I told you it was not a drug, it was totally safe, not expensive, and had no side effects, would you take it now? You might still be a little skeptical, you might think I'm a crank because it sounds too good to be true. But how about if I told you that world-class science supports the effectiveness of the substance, now would you take it? Probably, yes. It would seem crazy not to.

So, does this miracle substance really exist?

Yes, it does.

While I was writing this book, the research team at the University of Otago in New Zealand announced the results of a major study. And I do mean a major study. We see research studies reported all the time in the press, often contradictory and confusing. However, Otago was a real benchmark study, commissioned by the World Health Organization, that will no doubt influence the nutritional advice we will be given over the coming years.

The researchers analyzed 40 years of information on this substance and the results of 243 studies and clinical trials using thousands of people. This showed "a 15 to 30 percent decrease in deaths and incidence of coronary heart disease, stroke, type 2 diabetes and colorectal cancer" in people who took sufficient quantities of the substance. That is massively impressive. No drug can come even close to producing such amazing results.

So, what is this magic substance that could save your life? In fact, you eat it already, but if you eat a typical western diet, you probably don't eat anywhere near enough of it. According to the renowned medical journal The Lancet in the United Kingdom, for example, only 9% of the population eat enough. We are talking about nothing more than humble dietary fiber.

Fiber-rich foods pack an awesome nutritional punch because they are also the kinds of foods that are high in all the other good stuff your body needs, like vitamins, minerals, antioxidants, and phytochemicals. So, by taking the easy step of just focusing on getting more fiber in your diet, you make a huge overall difference to the quality of your diet and your health. It's an easy-to-follow, low-maintenance, high-reward strategy that you can put in place right now and change your life today. It's a no-brainer.

The research recommends at least 25 grams of fiber daily, and 30 grams would be better. Fibre comes from those good carbohydrates we discussed in the last chapter: wholegrain bread and pasta, vegetables of all descriptions, fruits, beans, peas, lentils, oats, and nuts.

To give you an idea of what this means, here are some examples. A medium potato in its skin would give you 4 grams of fiber; a pear would give you 5 grams; a cup of whole-wheat pasta would give you 6 grams; a cup of baked beans would give you 10 grams; a cup of split peas would give you 16 grams. By comparison, the cheeseburger we talked about in the last chapter would give you just one pathetic gram of fiber. These are just a few examples. You can find many lists of fiber-rich foods online. The

Mayo Clinic's website has a good list, just type "mayo clinic fiber" into Google.

Foods that are poor in fiber and other nutrients are those processed carbohydrates we looked at in the last chapter that have been stripped of their nutrients, like white bread and white pasta. It's important to look for whole grains.

Another outrageously easy health hack is boosting your intake of antioxidants, which help to slow down aging and combat major diseases. Fruit and vegetables are again the main sources of these, but the hack is to go for fruit and vegetables that are darker in color. The reason is that antioxidants add color to food, so the darker colors will contain larger amounts of antioxidants.

Therefore, dark purple romaine lettuce will be more beneficial than pale-green iceberg lettuce, dark red grapes are better than light green grapes, red potatoes are better than white potatoes, and so on. Colorful beans and peas of all types are great. Berries are fantastic, and bright red strawberries are bursting with antioxidants, but the dark color rule still applies, so darker blueberries will trump strawberries.

Pale fruits are still worth eating as they have other nutrients – I wouldn't want to stop eating apples or bananas. But the reason why apples start to go a rusty color if you cut one open and leave it exposed to the air is that it is oxidizing due to its lower antioxidant content. That wouldn't happen with an orange or a mango. So if you eat an apple, eat the skin, which is where the antioxidants will be concentrated.

Following a diet based on whole grains, vegetables, pulses, fruit and nuts is healthy. But how exactly do you know that it's working? A healthy diet reduces the chance of you contracting a horrible disease. But on a day-to-day basis, if you stay disease-free, you don't know if it has worked or not. You might not have got a disease anyway. So how do you know healthy eating works?

I know it works because I have been following this style of eating for several years and have seen the results. I'm not a saint. I love my food. I eat some processed food, for instance, but I limit it, and I never eat processed meat products. I think 90% of my diet could be classed as healthy.

I know that my high-nutrient, low-fat diet works because in the last few years, I haven't had any illnesses: no colds, sore throats, coughs, or cold sores on my lips. I used to get these things regularly. But I haven't had any since I changed my diet. The only logical explanation for this is the food I eat. Nothing else is different. I am not taking any medication. I don't take supplements. It must be diet.

This makes sense because the food I eat is constantly releasing high levels of nutrients into my body that boost my immune system, and that's what fights off illness. Sometimes I feel I have a cold or sore throat coming on, but then the symptoms vanish again before the illness develops. That's my immune system kicking in. And logically, if it keeps off the small illnesses, it will give me a better chance of keeping more serious illnesses at bay as well.

On top of that, I have also been able to measure the effects of my change in diet scientifically, using data from my annual health check. I have been tracking the test numbers for several years. They show that since making my diet change, my blood pressure and cholesterol readings have fallen from worryingly high levels to optimal, safe levels.

The difference is entirely due to diet changes. I take no drugs. It seems ridiculous to me that drug companies make mega-billions out of selling statins, for example, when simple changes in diet are far more effective, cheap, and have no side effects.

The benefits of changing to a healthy diet are vast. Recent research shows that all of the common diseases that we suffer from in the western world can be treated, and even reversed, through diet change. It's not difficult to do, either. This begs the question, why doesn't everyone do it?

Partly, this is due to a lack of information: the word is still getting out there. But many people are enormously resistant to changing from the junk food diet that is killing us in the west. We saw in the chapter about Terry why this is. As we discussed in the last chapter, processed foods, in particular, are addictive. They are designed to be so. The companies who make them want you to be hooked on the tastes. It's all about profit. And, as you now know from reading this book, addicted people see their information through a filter: they see what they want to see, and the rest is filtered out.

But you don't need to be addicted to this or anything else, because you know the power of having a Path.

The other main hack for health that I focus on is building incidental exercise into my day. Only this morning, Britain's Guardian newspaper, which isn't known for being sensationalist, ran a story headlined: Sitting down for too long may be causing 70,000 UK deaths a year.

What I mean by incidental exercise is keeping on the move as much as possible as part of your normal day rather than, say, going to the gym occasionally, or doing all your exercise all in one go, once a week. In the study of longevity known as the Blue Zones, researchers looked for similarities in the lifestyles of societies around the world that live the longest. One of their findings was that in long-lived societies, people had naturally active lives. They walked a lot as part of their normal day and had routine manual activities that kept their bodies moving.

This is an issue for me, as writing is a sedentary business. So, I look for little opportunities to get some more movement in my day. Nowadays, I avoid using my car as much as possible. If I can walk, I walk. There are all sorts of little hacks you can build into your life. For instance, if you can do your food shopping in bits and pieces every day, walking to the supermarket, you will get a lot more incidental exercise than loading up the car once a week.

One other thing that the Blue Zones researchers found was that all the longest-lived societies on earth had diets that were high in nutrient-rich, plant-based foods, just like we have been discussing over the last couple of chapters. So put that way of eating together with incidental exercise, and you have a winning combination that will keep you as healthy as your genetics will allow.

A lifestyle like this will also result in your feeling happier. We all want happiness. So next, we'll look at how to get more of that.

Happiness by Design

Wouldn't it be great if you knew the secret of happiness? Then you could use it to design a happy life. Sounds idyllic, doesn't it? But surely, it's not possible. If you Google happiness, you will come up will a huge variance in what people believe it is. What makes one person happy doesn't cut it for someone else. There is no common denominator. We are all so different. So, it would seem there can't be just one secret.

But maybe there is – and science can point us in the right direction.

We discussed neurotransmitters in the chapter on addiction, and dopamine in particular. Neurotransmitters are chemical messengers that whizz around your brain all the time, taking information from one place to another. Dopamine gives you a short-term feeling of pleasure. It's the source of the feeling of pleasure that Terry got when he experienced a favorite taste. Dopamine encourages you to want more, which is why it has a link to addiction.

But it's not the only neurotransmitter. Serotonin is another, and it's rather like the other side of the coin to dopamine. Serotonin also feels good, but it isn't short-term and addictive. Instead, it gives a longer-lasting feeling of happiness. Perhaps, indeed, serotonin is happiness.

Therefore, if serotonin makes you happy and you knew how to generate it, you could be happy by design.

Sounds good. Let's look deeper.

Serotonin is associated with positive moods, social behavior, good appetite, digestion, sleep, and sexual desire. Lack of serotonin, however, is associated with anxiety, poor sleeping patterns, low self-esteem, and even depression. In fact, the most common drugs for treating low mood and depression are called Selective Serotonin Reuptake Inhibitors, or SSRIs, which work by boosting your serotonin levels. These include well-known drugs such as Citalopram, Fluoxetine and Sertraline. If you've ever been prescribed Prozac, you were taking an SSRI.

But you don't need to take a drug to boost your serotonin and your happiness. There are simple actions you can take that will achieve the same result.

Exposure to natural light is up there at the top of the list. It's no coincidence that people are more likely to suffer from low mood and depression in the winter. So, making the most of the available daylight is the place to start if it's in short supply where you are right now.

166

Exercise is a major serotonin booster. And as a bonus, exercise also releases another neurotransmitter, endorphins, which is like natural morphine: it helps reduce pain and also prevents anxiety.

Meditation also boosts serotonin. If you think meditation is some sort of mystic voodoo, it's time to take off the filter and look again. I know you've probably been bombarded with articles about mindful meditation over the last few years, and if you've never tried it, you might be sick of hearing about it. But it works and science backs it up.

Mindfulness, as it is used nowadays in the West, was pioneered in the 1980s at the University of Massachusetts Medical School for stress reduction and chronic pain management. In the United Kingdom, the National Health Service has recommended mindfulness for anxiety relief since 2005, saying it is at least as effective as medication like SSRIs. If you haven't used mindfulness before and would like to have a go, please visit my website WinsPress.com, where you can read free samples of several mindfulness books and download free meditations.

I had a first-hand opportunity to put all this to the test a few years ago. I was back in England after several years away and was suddenly hit by a low mood at the start of the winter. My doctor diagnosed Seasonally Adjusted Disorder, a kind of depression brought on by lack of sunlight. It's really weird: it's like a switch has been flipped in your head in November, then turns off again just as suddenly in the spring.

Winter days in England are short and there's a lot of cloudy weather, so you can go days without even seeing the sun. At the time, I was working in a hospital. The sun was only just getting up as I arrived at work, and by the time I left, it was already dark.

Never having had any kind of depression before, it was a shock. My doctor prescribed a low-dosage SSRI. I am reluctant to take meds, but I felt I couldn't work with clients who were suffering from mood disorders themselves if I was, too. So, I took the medication. It worked, and then as soon as the sun came out three months later, I was absolutely fine and stopped taking them.

The following winter, it happened again. I took the medication again, but this time it didn't work. I don't know why, but I felt awful, worse than ever. My doctor suggested trying something else until we found a drug that suited me. But I decided to take a whole new approach, with no meds. I did my research, got a plan, and then started on a Path for the winter, taking Daily Action.

Firstly, I maximized the amount of time I spent in the daylight. Every lunchtime, I got out of the hospital and went walking to soak up whatever light was available.

Secondly, I got exercise. I parked a mile from the hospital on my way to work and walked the rest of the way. That way, combined with the lunchtime walking, I was walking several miles a day. At the weekend I got out as much as I could.

Thirdly, I listened to mindful recordings in the morning and evening. I also attended mindfulness groups and took part in an eight-week course.

It worked. The combination of the above activities kept the seasonal depression at bay until the sun returned in the spring. True, it would have been much easier to have simply taken a pill, as doing it my way was a lot of effort. But I had no unwanted side effects, and I feel that I changed my life for the better. I have never suffered much from Seasonally Adjusted Disorder since then. But if it does return, or if life becomes demanding in any other way, I now have mindfulness as a skill to fall back on.

There are other ways to boost your happiness by design.

Serotonin likes you to feel valued. If you don't feel that way, I suggest going back to the chapter Achievement Stacking. That's a great way to boost your feelings of confidence and self-esteem.

Serotonin rewards you for being sociable. Dopamine will give you a short-term buzz for doing something self-indulgent. But serotonin will give you long-term feelings of satisfaction for being part of a group and participating in your society.

Serotonin will reward you for giving. Dopamine will give you a short-term hit for grabbing something for yourself. But for long-lasting feelings of wellness, try giving of yourself. Take another look at what we were saying about being of service to others. I get a great feeling of warmth and pride looking back on the work I've done to help people and serve them to the best of my ability.

Serotonin will work its magic for you if you have a belief you can follow. This could be a secular philosophy, a religion, a lifestyle choice like yoga, or a political calling: anything that helps you to make sense of your world in those moments when your mind starts ruminating on the life questions that none of us can answer.

And Serotonin will also reward you for having a Path, focusing on your Daily Action, and being open about the outcomes. You will be calm and assured if you take this approach to life's opportunities and challenges.

Dreams by Choice

Early in this book, I wrote that I was living my dream, not by chance but by choice.

Now it's your turn.

You have learned how to see clearly what your greatest desires are.

You now know the simple power of creating a Path and using a Daily Action to take you to your goal.

You have learned how to defeat procrastination by not waiting till you're ready and can call up motivation anytime through taking a small action to create momentum.

You now understand that you can achieve even greater things than you planned by being open about your outcomes.

You know that recording the stats and cultivating cheerleaders will help you onwards, and you can empower yourself through achievement stacking and taking responsibility for your reactions to other people and events.

You've discovered how to succeed through giving service and using your imagination to create something out of nothing.

You have learned how to overcome addictions, anxiety, and self-defeating thought traps, such as mental filters and thinking that doing the same thing will give a different result.

You know simple hacks to help you have a healthy mind and body, and you can create happiness by taking simple actions.

You have everything you need to turn your dreams into a reality.

Except for one thing.

You need to take some action.

Right now.

None of what you have read will help you if you don't use it, and if you wait, you will give that voice in your head a chance to undermine you. It will try to convince you that you don't need to act today. It will suggest that perhaps you had better wait until Monday, or until your birthday, or until New Year, or until Jupiter is in your birth sign, or whatever excuse it can think of, to prevent your embracing change. It will tell you that you don't know enough yet and that you need to do more research and read more books.

But you don't.

You are already holding the book that you needed all along.

Take an action, take yourself by surprise, and trample that voice of self-doubt underfoot as you run down the Path that leads to your dream.

Thank You

That brings us to the end of Change Your Life Today. Thank you so much for joining me on the journey through this book.

But don't close this book yet. There is more!

I have added a bonus chapter, so read on...

Bonus Chapter

The following is a chapter from my book

The Emotional Mind: Overcome Anxiety, Stress, Negativity & Procrastination.

I hope you enjoy it.

In Two Minds.

When we are undecided, we sometimes say we are in two minds. This is an accurate explanation of how things are. In your head, you have a logical mind and an emotional mind.

I mean this literally.

Your logical mind is located at the front of your brain. You actively engage with it, so you are aware that you are thinking. As I write this book, my logical mind is fully engaged. If I get stuck about what to write next, I will consciously use my logical mind to find a way forward. It's this part of your brain that sets humans apart from other species because it gives us the ability to use imagination and solve problems. Where nothing previously existed, we can conceive an idea and then find a way to make it real.

If you look around, you can see the results of our imagination everywhere: the town you live in, the car you drive, the building you call home, the clothes you wear, the furniture you are relaxing on at this very moment. In the past, all these things were no more than someone's vision. A short time ago, this book only existed in my imagination, but now you are reading it. That conscious part of our brain has shaped our world – but it's not the most powerful part of your mind.

Your emotional mind is located farther back in your head. You don't consciously engage with it. Instead, it engages with you and, unlike your logical side, which switches off when you sleep, the emotional mind runs all the time. As soon as you doze off for a second, it takes centre-stage in your dreams. It works on a subconscious level, all the time monitoring your world, processing the information you are constantly collecting through your senses and sending you thoughts and feelings in a never-ending stream.

If you are watching a movie, the way you feel about the characters will change continuously as the plot unfolds and you learn more about them. You might start off disliking a character but end up loving them after your feelings have gone through all shades of opinion. You don't consciously keep thinking, "Do I like these characters?" You don't need to, because your emotional mind is constantly re-testing the information it receives about them. In the real world also, you are endlessly evaluating how you feel about every person you know – even your feelings about those you truly love will fluctuate within a range.

It's not just people. Your emotional mind crunches every bit of data your senses bring in, forming instant opinions and then firing them out at you in the form of thoughts and feelings, even while you sleep. Have you ever gone to bed feeling cheerful, only to feel like your world has ended in the morning? Your mood has collapsed overnight for no reason that you know. You go through your morning routine feeling like something awful has happened, although nothing has. Then suddenly, for no obvious reason, your mood lifts. What was that all about? Well, no doubt your emotional mind had changed its ideas about how it interpreted the world while you were asleep, but you didn't know until you woke up.

You cannot control the emotional mind in the same way you can your logical side, as it is in charge, subconsciously manipulating your emotional landscape. We try to control it with logic and can have some limited success, but it requires great effort and usually feels like you are holding back a dam that at some point is going to burst – it's just a question of time.

This is why we struggle with willpower. How many times have you decided to change a behaviour to improve yourself, such as going on a diet, only for your willpower to fall apart? You might keep going on willpower for a few days, but if your emotional mind is screaming: "Gimme, gimme!" every time you go near the kitchen, your resolve will eventually crumble.

Your emotional mind is too powerful for your logical side. Sometimes it seems like comparing the power of a modern computer to an old-fashioned pocket calculator. If you leave it to run the show, as most people do, you can expect your moods to go up and down constantly, stress and anxiety will be with you most of the time, and your feelings will run your life. But if this all sounds all gloom and doom, don't worry. Solutions exist, and they aren't complicated.

Imagine your emotions are being run by a computer at the back of your head. Now, think about this for a moment: you can re-program computers to work as you want, so why not your emotions? Imagine getting the power of your emotions working for you, instead of shoving you around randomly.

Well, you can.

Your emotional mind is reacting to the data it's picking up from your senses. It will be aware of every sound and smell in your environment far more than you are on a conscious level. It will monitor everything you see in minute detail and at colossal speed. It will pick up on slight changes in temperature, amounts of ambient light, and air movement on your skin. All this information and more is being mashed through and fed back to you as to how it thinks you should feel.

You might expect me to discuss ways of dealing with those feelings – and we will do that in this book – but that's looking at the data that are coming out of your brain in the form of feelings. How about taking a step back first and looking at the data that's going in? That's where you can make a difference simply and quickly.

Look at how you are physically right now. Let's start with your temperature – are you cold, or too hot, or just okay? Are you sitting somewhere comfortably? Is the lighting suitable for reading this book? If these basics are not right, your emotional brain will dislike the data it's picking up from your senses and will start sending you feelings that say you are unhappy. It will do this by sending you negative thoughts and shutting off the supply of your brain's natural feel-good chemicals, like dopamine and serotonin.

What you put into your mind via your senses directly affects the feelings you are getting out. If you input negative sensations into your emotional mind, you will get negative feelings coming out.

That is something you can deliberately change.

Classic things to look out for are if you are hungry, angry, lonely, or tired. If one of those applies, then take action. Eat if you are hungry, put on some relaxing music if you are angry, call your best friend if you are lonely, or go to bed if you are tired.

Maybe you need a change of environment. If you get out of the space you are in, your senses will be awash with new incoming data for your mind to analyse. If it likes the data it's receiving, it will send you approving thoughts and turn up the supply of the feel-good chemicals in your head.

So next time you feel low for no reason, instead of feeling sorry for yourself and getting into a downward spiral, deliberately ask yourself how you can change the data your senses are picking up. Otherwise, you could convince yourself that you are depressed when all you need to do is to turn on the heating, increase the light levels, change the music, or have a snack.

So today, when you have a negative feeling, instead of reacting emotionally, as you usually do, I want you to try something different: use negative thoughts as an opportunity to learn a new skill. Deliberately engage your logical mind. Try looking at your situation and ask yourself what information your emotional brain is absorbing from your environment via your senses. Is there something it would find objectionable? Think analytically about what you could change, then take action.

This will take a certain amount of concentration on your part, or you will immediately react as normal. This is why simply reading this book is insufficient. You need to actively try out the suggestions, or your autopilot will kick in, you will forget what you have read, and make no progress.

So, I suggest you task yourself with identifying 3 times today when a negative thought or feeling hits you and use the above exercise. It doesn't have to be a dramatically negative emotion: a simple feeling of discomfort is enough to use to get the hang of this way of thinking. What it will show you is that when you have a feeling, you have choices.

A negative thought or feeling is not a command for you to act negatively – it is an emotion, and emotions are not commands, they are merely passing events in your mind.

You can act on them if you wish, or you can choose to change the information going into your emotional brain, which will alter the feelings that come out.

Your emotional brain will reward you for feeding it more acceptable data because the good news about that part of your mind is that it gives you all your emotions, not just the toxic ones. It's where your happiness comes from as well. You will have a more contented life if you pay attention to what you feed it.

Most people go through life unaware that they have choices in how they respond to their emotions and that they can deliberately take action to affect the feelings your emotional mind throws out. If you were one of those people, you have just learned a major insight into your inner-self which, on its own, will make a huge difference to your life if you use it.

If you liked the bonus chapter from *The Emotional Mind* and would like to read more, please use this link to visit the book's Amazon page: viewbook.at/emotionalmind

Or if you want to check out all my books, free resources and downloads, please visit WinsPress.com

And if you enjoyed *Change Your Like Today*, I would be massively grateful if you could take a couple of minutes to leave a review on Amazon.

I wish you all the very best,

Lewis David.

Printed in Great Britain
by Amazon

35766319R00103